SPYCRAFT
for
Thriller Writers

How to Write Spy Novels, TV Shows and Movies Accurately and Not Be Laughed at by Real-Life Spies

EDWARD MICKOLUS

WW
WANDERING
WOODS
PUBLISHERS

Spycraft for Thriller Writers:
How to Write Spy Novels, TV Shows and Movies Accurately
and Not Be Laughed at by Real-Life Spies

By Edward F. Mickolus, PhD

First Edition February 2021

ISBN-13: 978-1-949173-06-2

Published in the United States by Wandering Woods Publishers

Book Design, Cover and Typesetting by
Cynthia J. Kwitchoff (CJKCREATIVE.COM)

WANDERING
WOODS
PUBLISHERS

DISCLAIMER

```
... / .--. / -.-- / -.-. / .--. / .- / ..-.
/ - / ..-. --- .-. / - / .... / .-. / .. /
.-.. / .-.. / . / .-. / .-- / .-. / .. / - /
. / .-. / ... / -... / -.-- / . / -.. / .-- /
.- / .-. / -.. / -- / .. / -.-. / -.- / --- /
.-.. / ..- / ... (delete the /s)
```

"Spy fiction, however many shots ring out, is always neat and tidy; the facts or espionage are quite the opposite. It is abundant in loose ends, false starts, and in incidents that are never quite rounded off."

—FORMER SIS OFFICER DAVID WALKER, 1957,
CITED IN *WEST, FABER BOOK OF ESPIONAGE*, 1993

"I fear that James bond in real life would have had a thick dossier in the Kremlin after his first exploit and would not have survived the second."

—FORMER DCI ALLEN DULLES,
GREAT SPY STORIES FROM FICTION, 1969

"Nothing I write is authentic."

—JOHN LE CARRE,
CNN.COM, DECEMBER 26, 2000

TABLE OF CONTENTS

$// \oplus //$

"I suspect that CIA more than perhaps any institution in America has been subject to mythology and misinformation. The result of too many novels, too may television shows, too many conspiracy theorists, too many James Bond and Jack Ryan movies…"

—Former DCI Robert Gates, 1999

"Best-sellers… ignore the fact that the purpose behind the imagined hugger-mugger involved in secret intelligence collection is to keep national policymakers well enough informed to make sound decisions and to avoid catastrophic mistakes."

—Former DCI Richard Helms,
A Look Over My Shoulder, 2003

INTRODUCTION

Much of what the public believes it understands about espionage in general and the CIA in particular, and anything in between, comes from spy fiction (spy-fi): novels, television series, and movies. Sometimes the writers get it right. More often, they do not, to the detriment of the public's understanding of what intelligence officers do for our country, the development of misimpressions at home and overseas of the missions and operations of these organizations, and a winnowing of the number of talented people who would otherwise consider a career in intelligence. Intelligence is one of the world's oldest professions, and possibly the most misunderstood.

When I joined the U.S. Central Intelligence Agency more than 40 years ago, television and movies had been in a golden age of spy-fi. James Bond reigned supreme, but a host of other notional spies skulked solidly behind him. We thrilled to the exploits of such heroes as Napoleon Solo and Illya Kuriakin (The Man from U.N.C.L.E.), the team from Mission Impossible (since reduced in the movie series to Tom Cruise's Ethan Hunt character and his supporting cast), Matt Helm, Derek Flint, Modesty Blaise, Honey West, James West and Artemus Gordon, The Prisoner, Kelly Robinson and Alexander Scott.

Later years brought us the other JBs—Jack Bauer and Jason Bourne and the almost-JB Jack Ryan—plus Austin Powers, Johnny English, Chuck, and Archer. The role of women has advanced from the at-best sidekicks of Emma Peel and Agent 99 to Carrie Mathison, Sidney Bristow, Annie Walker, Nikita, Salt, Lorraine Broughton, and Elizabeth Jennings. Many of these characters grew from novels.

Spies in novels and on screen often are portrayed as clever and amoral assassins, sometimes going rogue to do battle with bureaucracies that have metastasized into evil versions of their real-world models. They often are loners, jetting off to far-flung countries at a moment's notice, with no developed "backstopping" of their cover identities. Often they simply announce themselves in their true names, and expect the bad guys to know who they are and that they have met their match. They often have intriguing gadgets, be it an Aston Martin DB-5, the Man from U.N.C.L.E.'s multi-version gun, or Maxwell Smart's various Cones of Silence. Their enemies frequently capture them, then subject them and/or their associates to physical and mental tortures, but ultimately blab away the details of their nefarious plans and reveal the fatal flaw. The good guys always figure things out in time and save the world, with a maximum of quips, gunfire, explosions, and sex.

Although the primary focus of spy-fi, as well as my career, was on the Central Intelligence Agency (CIA), I have included discussion of the rest of the Intelligence Community (IC), including their locations (so that you don't have your protagonist simply walking across the street from one agency to another), photos of their headquarters buildings, principal seals/logos, and their mission(s) within the Executive Branch. I have included a more extensive treatment of the Federal Bureau of Investigation (FBI), where I taught tradecraft and which seems to have a spy-fi focus second only to that of CIA.

This volume will give you tips on how we go about our work, what some of our arcane language means, and what we are like. It will point out common myths, and suggest how you can avoid perpetuating their more deleterious effects on your credibility and our public images.

Working on the assumption that I have not cornered the market on insights into this topic, I conferred with hundreds of members of the Intelligence Community, many of whom preferred to not be named, some of whom have worked with spy-fi authors who sometimes chose to incorporate their counsel, sometimes did not. Thanks to them—they know who they are and you don't have to—along with Lanie D'Alessandro, Beth Barns, Bill Barrett, Stephanie Bellistri, Mark Benbow, Darrell Blocker, Diana Bolsinger, Kip Brailey, Andrea Hattler Bramson, Thomas Leo Briggs, Terry Joseph Busch, Kevin Callahan, Gary Carroll, Leo Chambliss, Clint Collins, Nicholas Dujmovic, Robert Eatinger, Ron Estes, Rodney Faraon, Lia Fidas, Bob Flores, Dennis Gleeson, Anne Gruner, Jay Grusin, John Hedley, Courtney Runion Hunt, Elinor Houghton Kelly, Martha Neff Kessler, Phil Lago, Darryl Lansey, Spencer Lee, Irma Lopez, Clint Mesle, Chan Mohney, John Nolton, Jon Nowick, Mary O'Sullivan, Hugh Pettis, Robert Phillipson, Will Rogers, Ross Stapleton-Gray, Janet Stiegler, Michael Sulick, Gerhardt Thamm, Kathleen Bardzell Thomas, Mike Toth, Bo Tumasz, Tom Weber, Raymond Wong, Debra Yamanaka, and Donna Zerbato. You'll find their insights sprinkled throughout these pages. I have, however, cornered the market on errors in this book.

This book is not designed to be a comprehensive primer on how to conduct intelligence collection and covert action operations, perform analysis, provide intelligence to customers, or run the organizations. There are other sources you can consult, including the organizations' websites and many books in the Further Reading section at the end of this volume.

I am not going to expose sensitive clandestine sources and methods here. Rather, this book covers the types of material that my colleagues and I frequently see in fictional writing about espionage, and will lead you away from some of the more common glaring errors. It will give you just what you need to provide an accurate flavor of where we work, what we do, how we sound, how we think, and what motivates us. You can improve the accuracy of your writing and eliminate unintentionally irritating slurs against American patriots by paying careful attention to these observations.

//⊕//

WEBSITE: intelligence.gov

THE INTELLIGENCE COMMUNITY'S MEMBER ORGANIZATIONS: LOGOS, LOCATIONS, MISSIONS

The Intelligence Community is composed of 16 Executive Branch member organizations, plus the Office of the Director of National Intelligence. Under the National Security Act of 1947, a Director of Central Intelligence (DCI), in addition to running the CIA, was also the President's chief intelligence advisor and led the Intelligence Community. Since the Intelligence Reform and Terrorism Prevention Act of 2004, the latter two duties have been given to the Senate-confirmable Director of National Intelligence (DNI).

The members of the IC agencies frequently communicate with each other, sharing information and insights over computer systems and classified social media. Its online Intellipedia facilitates collaborative data sharing via three wikis running on the separate JWICS (Intellipedia-TS),

SIPRNet (Intellipedia-S), and DNI-U (Intellipedia-U) networks. These systems are devoted to, respectively, Top Secret, Secret, and Unclassified materials. It is not available to the public. Officers communicate through unclassified and classified e-mail systems, instant messaging capabilities, and a classified version of Twitter called Chirp.

With the expansion of threats to the U.S. homeland, IC members often also communicate with state, local, and tribal authorities.

Except for the CIA, the member organizations of the IC report to a Cabinet secretary. The CIA Director (D/CIA) reports to the President via the Director of National Intelligence.

THE OFFICE OF THE DIRECTOR OF NATIONAL INTELLIGENCE (ODNI)

WEBSITE: ODNI.gov

The headquarters of ODNI is located at 1500 Tysons McLean Drive, McLean, Virginia.

The Director of National Intelligence (DNI) is a Cabinet-level official whose primary mission is to lead the IC in intelligence integration, in essence ensuring that the Community members are most efficiently allocating resources in collecting, analyzing, and providing intelligence to policymakers. The position has so far gone to civilians. ODNI's National Centers integrate and coordinate IC member activities, and in some cases, coordinate broader U.S. government activities in counterterrorism, counterproliferation, counterintelligence, and cyber.

Among the initiatives of ODNI is instituting a parallel to the military services' Goldwater-Nichols Act requirement that those hoping to advance to the seniormost ranks of the organization serve a tour outside of their agency. This earlier was called by FBI and CIA officers the "exchange of hostages" program. It has since become common for armed forces officers to "go purple" to get a broader perspective on the missions and capabilities of all of the armed forces, and for senior intelligence officers to serve tours outside of their agency, and sometimes out of the Intelligence Community itself.

THE DEFENSE SERVICE AGENCIES

The Pentagon is located in Arlington County, Virginia, across the Potomac River from Washington, D.C.

The mission of the Department of Defense (DoD) is to provide a lethal Joint Force to defend the security of our country and sustain American influence abroad.

The Service agencies each have their intelligence organizations, generally aimed at the tactical and strategic needs of their parent services. They attend meetings of the Intelligence Community, frequently liaise with other IC members, and participate in drafting National Intelligence Estimates, the key long-term estimative products of the Community.

DOD Photo By: Air Force Tech. Sgt. Ned T. Johnston

WEBSITE: ARMY.mil

WEBSITE: NAVY.mil

WEBSITE: MARINES.mil

Key terminology: Retired Marines are "former" Marines, never ex-Marines.

U.S. AIR FORCE

WEBSITE: AF.mil

WEBSITE: USCG.mil

The Coast Guard is one of the rare IC member organizations that has an intelligence charter but also arrest powers.

WEBSITE: SPACEFORCE.mil

Motto: Always Above. Employees are called "guardians"

UNITED STATES
SPACE FORCE

The Combat Support Agencies

The Office of the Secretary of Defense has an Under Secretary of Defense for Intelligence (USD(I)), who has broad authority over all of the military-specific intelligence services. In addition to the five service intelligence agencies noted earlier, USD(I) also provides oversight to the four combat support agencies, whose budgets fall under the Department of Defense.

DEFENSE INTELLIGENCE AGENCY (DIA)

WEBSITE: DIA.mil

DIA's headquarters is located on Joint Base Anacostia-Bolling, in Washington, D.C.

The Defense Intelligence Agency informs national civilian and defense policymakers about the military intentions and capabilities of foreign governments and non-state actors. It collects intelligence via military operations officers and defense attaches. DIA is the IC's focal point for measurement and signature intelligence (MASINT), a technical branch of intelligence gathering, which serves to detect, track, identify or describe the signatures (distinctive characteristics) of fixed or dynamic target sources. Its employees include military officers and civilians.

Photo from DIA website

WORKING AT DIA

NATIONAL SECURITY AGENCY (NSA)

WEBSITE: NSA.gov

The National Security Agency (NSA) headquarters building is located in Fort Meade, Maryland, a non-trivial drive from downtown Washington, D.C.

The National Security Agency/Central Security Service leads the U.S. Government in cryptology that encompasses both signals intelligence (SIGINT) and information assurance (now referred to as cybersecurity) products and services, and enables computer network operations (CNO) in order to gain a decision advantage for the Nation and our allies under all circumstances. Note that it does not have arrest powers, a frequent error in espionage fiction. It does not have the time, mission, or inclination to spy on any random American that wanders by. Its officers do not conduct human source operations.

Photo from NSA website

NATIONAL GEOSPATIAL INTELLIGENCE AGENCY (NGA)

WEBSITE: NGA.mil

NGA's headquarters is located in Springfield, Virginia, with a major facility in St. Louis, Missouri.

NGA delivers geospatial intelligence (GEOINT) to policymakers, warfighters, intelligence professionals and first responders. It provides mapping and overhead photographic services for other IC members and policymakers.

Photos from https://www.callisonrtkl.com/projects/national-geospatial-intelligence-agency-campus-east-nga/

NATIONAL RECONNAISSANCE OFFICE (NRO)

WEBSITE: NRO.gov

The NRO headquarters building is at 14675 Lee Road, Chantilly, Virginia.

Formed in response to the Soviet launch of Sputnik, the NRO was secretly created on September 6, 1961 with the purpose of overseeing "all satellite and overflight reconnaissance projects whether overt or covert". Simply put, it launches the satellites with sensors that provide raw technical intelligence to the IC, mostly NGA and NSA.

NRO at 50 Years: A Brief History
https://www.nro.gov/Portals/65/documents/history/csnr/programs/NRO_Brief_History.pdf

THE DEPARTMENT OF JUSTICE AGENCIES

FEDERAL BUREAU OF INVESTIGATION (FBI)

WEBSITE: FBI.gov

As of this writing, the FBI's headquarters building is 935 Pennsylvania Ave, NW, Washington, D.C. A common Washington topic for discussion is where a new headquarters facility should be located. The FBI's famed training facility is located on a Marine base in Quantico, Virginia. Much training is conducted on the fictitious street of Hogan's Alley. FBI trainees wear distinctive color-coded polo shirts, indicating their area of expertise, including special agents, analysts, and financial specialists.

The FBI has been America's principal federal law enforcement (LE) agency since the 1920s. In the wake of the 9/11 attacks, it acquired a more

FBI Headquarters building, courtesy of the FBI and Library of Congress

FBI Academy Hogan's Alley photo courtesy of the FBI.

proactive mission, adding intelligence operational and analytic duties to its LE activities. Now in addition to developing cases to prosecute in court against specific criminal offenses that have taken place, the Bureau also works on preventing terrorist attacks. Terrorism has also been named its top investigative priority. Other key areas of investigation are counterintelligence, cyber crime, public corruption, civil rights, organized crime, white-collar crime, violent crime, and weapons of mass destruction.

FBI special agents, after their training at Quantico, are assigned a badge and a gun. Other FBI officers do not have the means of lethal force, nor arrest powers. Special agents are assigned to FBI field offices, now called Divisions. FBI Headquarters also has Divisions devoted to specific topics. Supervisory special agents oversee operations of special agents, who initially work in small teams called squads. Larger groups are called units. The Bureau also runs Joint Terrorism Task Forces which are based throughout the United States. Special agents assigned overseas work in legal attache offices in U.S. embassies, liaising with local law enforcement in the country of assignment.

FBI employees work on topics, often referred to as domains. They can include geographic regions, as well as terrorism, counterintelligence, cyber crime, public corruption, civil rights, organized crime, white-collar crime, violent crime, and weapons of mass destruction.

FBI patois includes adding "Bu" as a prefix to common words. A quasi-personal vehicle, which in CIA parlance would be a QPV, in Bureau-speak is a BuCar.

One should pay careful attention to the different cultures of the Intelligence Community agencies, and not conflate, say, CIA and FBI. An FBI colleague notes differences in the two organizations. "In general, I take issue with Hollywood's presentation of our work. Sets (offices) are stylized with a group of agents sitting in a gadget-loaded, well-appointed work space, under film noire lighting, discussing a single case and how to proceed with it. No writing and reports of course. And, all sexes and races are represented. Lots of quick, subsequent action.

"In reality, the opposite is true. Work areas are quite spartan, well-lit, sans fancy lighting, designer furniture, gadgets, and muffled voices. Most agents carry a case load—anywhere from 10 to 40 cases. Many years ago, agents could have upwards of 80 cases assigned. For example, one case for a targeted organization and 79 cases on each of the 79 members of the organization. Not a whole lot of time to sit around and philosophize. And we have reporting rules. Back when, circa 1970, we had to post each case, a minimum of 60 days.

"If there was a big spy case, usually an old head and a couple of his buddies handled it. Need to know and very hush hush. Never assigned to a newbie and never to a gaggle of agents described above. Files were sequestered, removed from common access and placed under lock and key. "For something very sensitive, we had off-sites and/or secure rooms within our office. These I would have to discuss with you in person.

"My best description of our work: 92% dogged research, interviews, surveillances, report writing, more report writing and answering bureaucratic queries; 6% excitement, arrests, chases, identification of targets, prevention of terrorist acts, convictions, etc.; and 2% pure terror, dangerous circumstances, shootings, etc. Cases may take years to handle."

Another FBI colleague counsels that
- When SWAT is used only SWAT members go in; all other agents stay away until the site is cleared.
- High profile searches are done by the ERT (evidence response team) which consists of agents and support personnel.
- An agent can have collateral duties, i.e., SWAT, ERT, assistant firearms instructor, EEO counselor, etc., but they are primarily a street agent.
- Agents volunteer to become supervisors; they are not necessarily the cream of the crop. Being a supervisor involves a lot more sitting behind a desk, being a street agent is more fun but less pay and less job opportunities after retirement.
- The vast majority of times the FBI and local law enforcement get along great, especially agents and detectives, the rare rift is usually among upper management on both sides. CIA-FBI relations are also generally cordial, despite media and spy-fi lore, and friendships can extend over decades.
- Major cases usually have more than one agent assigned, especially TIll cases, and they are called co-case agents.
- Agents normally do not travel outside their assigned territory to cover leads; they will send leads to the division responsible for that area.

Sub-cultures exist within the FBI, as they do within the CIA, and specific terminology is used by, say, special agents. In some instances, dialects develop within field offices/divisions. For example, the New York City field office referred to Soviet officials' wives as "alphas". Car surveillance was "sitting in the bucket". A "crystal room" is the equivalent of a Sensitive Compartmented Information Facility (SCIF).

DRUG ENFORCEMENT ADMINISTRATION (DEA)

WEBSITE: DEA.gov

DEA's headquarters building is located at 600 Army Navy Drive, Arlington, Virginia.

DEA's website notes that its mission is to enforce the controlled substances laws and regulations of the United States and bring to the criminal and civil justice system of the United States, or any other competent jurisdiction, those organizations and principal members of organizations, involved in the growing, manufacture, or distribution of controlled substances appearing in or destined for illicit traffic in the United States; and to recommend and support non-enforcement programs aimed at reducing the availability of illicit controlled substances on the domestic and international markets.

Photo appeared on DEA's www.campusdrugprevention.gov website.
Used with the permission of DEA's Office of Public Affairs

In carrying out its mission as the agency responsible for enforcing the controlled substances laws and regulations of the United States, the DEA's primary responsibilities include:

- Investigation and preparation for the prosecution of major violators of controlled substance laws operating at interstate and international levels.
- Investigation and preparation for prosecution of criminals and drug gangs who perpetrate violence in our communities and terrorize citizens through fear and intimidation.
- Management of a national drug intelligence program in cooperation with federal, state, local, and foreign officials to collect, analyze, and disseminate strategic and operational drug intelligence information.
- Seizure and forfeiture of assets derived from, traceable to, or intended to be used for illicit drug trafficking.
- Enforcement of the provisions of the Controlled Substances Act as they pertain to the manufacture, distribution, and dispensing of legally produced controlled substances.
- Coordination and cooperation with federal, state and local law enforcement officials on mutual drug enforcement efforts and enhancement of such efforts through exploitation of potential interstate and international investigations beyond local or limited federal jurisdictions and resources.
- Coordination and cooperation with federal, state, and local agencies, and with foreign governments, in programs designed to reduce the availability of illicit abuse-type drugs on the United States market through non-enforcement methods such as crop eradication, crop substitution, and training of foreign officials.
- Responsibility, under the policy guidance of the Secretary of State and U.S. Ambassadors, for all programs associated with drug law enforcement counterparts in foreign countries.
- Liaison with the United Nations, Interpol, and other organizations on matters relating to international drug control programs.

Along with the FBI, its agents have arrest powers and are authorized to carry firearms.

While novelists often refer to DEA agents as "narcs", a more accurate and less condescending term is DEA agents.

Note that it is Drug Enforcement Administration, not Agency.

Other Cabinet Agencies

STATE DEPARTMENT - BUREAU OF INTELLIGENCE AND RESEARCH (INR)

WEBSITE: STATE.gov/s/INR

The Department of State's Headquarters building is located at 2201 C Street, NW, Washington, D.C., in the Foggy Bottom area of Washington, a short walk from the Watergate Hotel and George Washington University.

Its small Bureau of Intelligence and Research lists its mission as harnessing intelligence to serve U.S. diplomacy. Secretary of State George Marshall established INR in 1947, the same year CIA was created. INR traces its roots to the WWII-era Office of Strategic Services Research Department.

Its website notes that drawing on all-source intelligence, INR provides value-added independent analysis of events to U.S. State Department policymakers; ensures that intelligence activities support foreign policy and national security purposes; and serves as the focal point in the State Department for ensuring policy review of sensitive counterintelligence and law enforcement activities around the world. The bureau directs the Department's program of intelligence analysis

and research, liaises with the Intelligence Community, and represents the Department on committees and in interagency intelligence groups. INR also analyzes geographical and international boundary issues.

INR all-source analysts focus primarily on supporting diplomats and diplomacy with a wide range of information and analyses. INR participates in the production of joint IC products, usually under the auspices of ODNI's National Intelligence Council (NIC), and in the drafting and coordinating of articles for the President's Daily Briefing (PDB). INR is the U.S. Government leader for foreign public opinion research and analysis.

The Department's protective service, the Diplomatic Security Service, is separate from INR.

U.S. diplomatic reporting can be used in all-source intelligence analysis, although State diplomats per se are not considered intelligence officers.

Shutterstock

DEPARTMENT OF THE TREASURY

WEBSITE: TREASURY.gov

The Department of the Treasury's headquarters building is located at 1500 Pennsylvania Avenue, NW, Washington, D.C., next to the White House.

The website notes that its small Office of Terrorism and Financial Intelligence (TFI) marshals the Department's intelligence and enforcement functions with the aims of safeguarding the financial system against illicit use and combating rogue nations, terrorist facilitators, weapons of mass destruction proliferators, money launderers, drug kingpins, and other national security threats. Treasury's all-source analysts develop background materials to support the naming by State and/ or Treasury of Specially Designated Global Terrorists under Executive Order 13224 that impose financial sanctions on violators.

Shutterstock

DEPARTMENT OF ENERGY

WEBSITE: ENERGY.gov

DOE's headquarters are located in the James V. Forrestal Building on Independence Avenue, SW, Washington, D.C., and in Germantown, Maryland.

DOE's Office of Intelligence and Counterintelligence is responsible for all intelligence and counterintelligence activities throughout the DOE complex, including nearly thirty intelligence and counterintelligence offices nationwide.

Shutterstock

DEPARTMENT OF HOMELAND SECURITY

WEBSITE: DHS.gov

The Department of Homeland Security's headquarters building is part of the Nebraska Avenue Complex located in southwest Washington, D.C., across from American University. There has been discussion in Washington of moving it elsewhere in the city. Its 180,000 employees belong to 22 offices, including

- Countering Weapons of Mass Destruction Office
- Federal Emergency Management Agency (FEMA)
- Federal Law Enforcement Training Centers (FLETC)
- Federal Protective Service (FPS)
- Office of Intelligence and Analysis
- Transportation Security Administration (TSA)
- U.S. Citizenship and Immigration Services (CIS)

Shutterstock

- U.S. Coast Guard (USCG), which retains a military capability
- U.S. Customs and Border Protection (CBP)
- U.S. Immigration and Customs Enforcement (ICE)
- U.S. Secret Service (USSS)

NT50s: Federal, State, Local, and Tribal

There are other government agencies, at all levels, that are not formally part of the Intelligence Community but nonetheless have interests in intelligence, sometimes as incidental collectors and often as consumers of intelligence, and which often liaise with IC members. They are called NT50s, so named for not being part of Title 50 of the U.S. Code of Federal Regulations on Intelligence, which covers war and national defense.

// ⊕ //

WEBSITE: CIA.gov

GETTING TO KNOW THE CIA

T he only Intelligence Community agency that is not part of a Cabinet department, it reports directly to the President via the Office of the Director of National Intelligence. Twice in its history the Agency's Director, then called the Director of Central Intelligence (DCI), and since the creation of ODNI, now the Director of the CIA (D/CIA), was a member of the Cabinet

TERMINOLOGY

"I could tell you, but then I'd have to kill you"—said no one at CIA, ever, to anyone. We've heard it before. It wasn't funny when someone coined it 60 years ago, and it's still not funny. Try to be original in your dialogue. Your readers will appreciate the effort, and the professionals will appreciate your avoidance of tired clichés.

HOW THINGS GET DONE: KEY CONCEPTS AND TERMS

Intelligence Cycle

There are several different formulations of the **Intelligence Cycle**, a continuous-loop feedback mechanism that ensures that intelligence professionals are providing useful intelligence to assist policymakers in their deliberations. For our purposes, we will look at Customer Questions, Requirements, Tasking, Collecting, Reporting, Analyzing, Writing/Briefing.

Customer Questions come about during briefings as well as from written comments, often scribbled on hardcopy (which still exist!) finished and raw intelligence reports and sent via classified electronic mail systems, and classified phone calls. Sometimes analysts can answer the question(s) immediately, sometime they need to draft a formal reply, and sometimes they say, "we don't know, but we will look into it and get back to you."

These latter replies lead to the development of intelligence **requirements** that IC members will use to guide the use of their collection and analytic resources. Collection specialists will work with all of the IC to determine which collection platforms, including human, are the most appropriate in obtaining intelligence to answer the customer questions. Offices within the Office of the Director of National Intelligence ensure that these efforts are integrated across the IC and that no requirements fall through the cracks because of "surges" to respond to urgent crises and/ or because agencies assumed that other services were handling the issue. These determinations are then translated into formal **tasking** to the various IC members, who have different terminology for their requirements lists.

The relevant **collectors** then obtain the intelligence and report it via their departmental channels to individuals who process the reports, evaluating the accuracy and plausibility of the reporting, searching for corroborating materials, and determining the sensitivity and dissemination of the reporting. **Analysts**, particularly all-source analysts at CIA and other

IC members, sift through the mountain of reports and attempt to make sense of the reporting using various structured analytical techniques. The analytic cadre then provides **finished intelligence** in the form of **written papers** (physical and digital) and **briefings** tailored to the specific needs of the policymakers. The policymakers in turn will have questions based upon these products, and the cycle begins anew.

One rarely sees this process in novels, tv show, or movies. Earlier spy-fi focused on catch-a-spy micro-level counterintelligence. Contemporary spy-fi follows covert action. Perhaps you could break new storytelling ground by showing mastery of the collection process, which is what most HUMINT officers do for their careers. As one of my colleagues observed,

> "I've often said to my students that moviemakers mostly make movies about cops, lawyers, doctors, the military and spies. The one thing they have in common is long periods of paperwork and preparation, with intermittent bursts of adrenalin. The difference is that all of those genres, except spies, contain elements that usually build to some kind of life-or-death climax that can be resolved in an hour or two. Our stories unfold over long periods of time and are better represented by the wheel we use to represent our acquisition cycle, which implies a continuum rather than a linear beginning, middle and end to the story that you can get with the other four genres. For this reason, writers have to make our stuff conform to the linear model to make it interesting to viewers/readers. And that's where it inevitably goes off the rails. The result is that most of the spy-centric stories are much further from reality than the others. Secrecy plays a part in that as well (unless you've done it and been on the inside, you can't really know what it is like), but less and less as more of our tradecraft leaks into the public domain. The real problem is fitting it into the increasing formulaic TV and cinema formats, which require car chases, explosions and shootouts. Never had any of those things happen, even though I had a pretty interesting career."

Agent Acquisition Cycle and Clandestine Service Team Members

Speaking of processes that receive short shrift in spy-fi treatments, the **Agent Acquisition Cycle** is often misrepresented, if downright ignored. Most assets (also known as agents or sources) are treated in spy-fi as if they are easily expendable individuals of whom there is an unlimited supply. The real story is far different, and intelligence assets are viewed as precious, deserving of every effort to protect their safety. That view in turn leads to the need-to-know principle, limiting the likelihood of leaking of the identities of assets.

Writers need to understand a critical difference in the potential uses of information from human sources. If one is obtaining information for **law enforcement**, one focuses upon making a case regarding one or more violations of criminal law. A prosecuting attorney will need to present **evidence** in open court, often relying upon individuals to identify themselves and testify in that court. The relationship between the law enforcement officer and the human source (often called **"informant"** or "cooperating informant", never to be denigrated as "snitch" or other derogatory term) can be fleeting, limited to what evidence the informant can provide relevant to a specific case. In some instances, the relationship can be longer term, with the informant providing law enforcement with a window on the criminal environment in which these violations occur.

The use of information obtained by intelligence officers from their human sources (**assets, agents, or sources**), called HUMINT (human intelligence), again drives the character of the officer-asset relationship. HUMINT is collected as part of the suite of methods used to obtain intelligence on a given topic—a government, an organization, an individual leader—to give policymakers our best analytic insights into the state of play on a topic, and our best estimate on what is likely to occur in the future and how other actors may react to policymakers' choices.

While the officer will still meet with the HUMINT source with the same level of clandestine tradecraft used with the law enforcement informant, the treatment of the intelligence information, and thus the length of the relationship, will differ. Intelligence officers are looking at the long term—the future—not what happened in an earlier criminal incident. HUMINT source reporting relationships can last for years, and in some cases, decades. Access to the HUMINT information is thus limited to a small group of intelligence officers and policymakers with a need to know the information, and is not intended to ever be used in court. Likewise, the identity of the HUMINT source is not to be revealed. Intelligence officers go to great lengths to fuzz the identity of their sources; the identity of the HUMINT source is separated from the substance of their reporting when disseminating their information to customers.

How intelligence officers go about collecting HUMINT is inherent in the Agent Acquisition Cycle, which includes Targeting, Spotting, Assessing, Developing, Recruiting, Handling, and Terminating the relationship.

Let's suppose that a policymaker expresses interest in knowing more about the nuclear weapons program of Ruritania. The Intelligence Community learns of this policymaker interest in a number of ways, such as formal tasking or questions raised during briefings.

A **targeter** (never "targeteer") determines what types of organizations are involved in the nuclear weapons program, and within that organization, what types of individuals (stated differently, what positions/job categories) might have access to the information in question. Generally, no one individual will have access to all of the information needed, but several individuals can provide different perspectives on the issue. The targeter then burrows down through the organization, determining which individuals (by name) might fulfill these collection needs. Targeters can be found in the analytic, operational, and science and technology directorates.

Meanwhile, the **operations officer** (earlier called case officer, never called case worker) is out meeting people in various fora, reporting back to Headquarters and asking for assistance in determining if these people s/he has **spotted** might be of interest as well. A **staff operations officer** does biographical intelligence research on these individuals, attempting to determine their access to intelligence information on the topic.

Once the individual has been deemed likely to have access, the station's team further **assesses** the individual's access and potential motivation to cooperate with the intelligence officer in providing that information.

The operations officer then **develops** a relationship of trust with the individual, befriending them, learning further about their access and motivation, and what needs in the individual's life are not being met by their family, caste, job, career, and society. The team will determine whether any of these needs can be met by the intelligence organization, and how the relationship can be developed from a one-on-one friendship to a more professional fealty to the organization per se.

As a senior colleague noted, "Once a foreign target has been met and agrees to meet a second time with an operations officer, he is generally referred to as a **contact** or 'early developmental.' At that point, the officer has virtually no control over the target except his agreement to meet again. The next phase in the cycle is to determine what access to secret intelligence the target actually has. At this stage, the officer will also work to develop a relationship of trust with the individual and gain understanding of him and his possible knowledge of secret activities of interest. The officer will also remain alert for possible financial or other vulnerabilities which the target exhibits or reveals.

If the operations officer reaches these goals with the individual, "the potential asset will then be categorized as a '**developmental**,' or, if the relationship progresses well, as an 'advanced developmental.' By now, the officer has gained some control over the target, as he now knows secret information which the developmental would want to keep from others. The target will now be accepting gifts, favors and/or money from the officer. He also must agree to meet clandestinely and to keep his relationship with the officer secret. The developmental is carefully "**vetted**" to confirm that he is who he says he is and legitimately has access to secret information. The Agency team might use audio, telephone taps, surveillance and access agents, among other things, to collect this information.

After the field and Headquarters assess that there is a reasonably good chance that the developmental would respond favorably to a request to wittingly provide secret intelligence in exchange for money or other inducements, the officer will develop a **pitch** to the individual, **recruiting** them to provide intelligence. The pitch puts the individual in their best light, making them the hero in their introspective story. They can see themselves as working for world peace, or for patriotic reasons, or for a better life for their children, or any combination of other altruistic purposes. If the individual agrees and then begins to provide that intelligence, the intelligence will be carefully evaluated and vetted. If the intelligence is deemed useful to the USG, the developmental may be recharacterized as an 'asset' or 'agent'.

There may be occasions in which the institutional affiliation of the operations officer will be obscured to the agent. This type of operation is called "false flagging", and is a technique found around the world by national intelligence services.

After a successful pitch, the relationship then becomes more clandestine, with the handling of their meetings being more security-focused. The safety of the asset and the security of the relationship is paramount, and much time is spent training the asset in clandestine tradecraft tailored to their personal situation and local environment. The asset—not the operations officer—physically obtains the intelligence information.

The operations officer then sends to Headquarters intelligence reports based upon the material provided by the asset. A **collection management officer** (earlier called reports officer or reports and requirements officer) vets the materials collected against previous reporting by the asset, its coherence with other sources, and a host of other considerations, then puts it into a format for dissemination to the analytic community and policymaker customers. **Analysts** then combine this reporting with that from other sources (e.g., signals, measurement and signatures, open source, photos, etc.) and using structured analytic techniques (designed to ensure rigor in critical thinking), write finished reports and present intelligence briefings.

At some point, the asset might be **'turned over'** to be handled by another operations officer. While turnovers regularly take place when operations officers depart their overseas post for another location, other turnovers are often designed to be another way to 'vet' the value of the asset and evaluate the level of control the Agency has over him.

Due to policymaker interest waning in a topic, or the asset losing access to intelligence on a topic due to new career circumstances, or a host of other reasons, the value of the asset on a particular topic may erode. Or the asset may have been compromised to a hostile intelligence service. Or the asset may have developed shoddy tradecraft, or a drinking problem, or be otherwise unreliable in the relationship. Any of these reasons may lead to the decision to end the clandestine contact, called **terminating** the relationship. This termination meeting is conducted in a friendly manner, but with the operations officer underscoring in a firm manner that the meeting is the final one that they will have. There is no "terminate with extreme prejudice."

Covert Action

Covert action is perhaps the least understood and most often ineptly-depicted aspect of intelligence work by authors.

Based upon the understanding of a situation a President has developed using, inter alia, the intelligence s/he has been provided, s/he may determine that a foreign country/organization is going in a direction inimical to U.S. interests. S/he can issue a **Presidential Finding** directing CIA to engage in specific types of actions designed to lead to a specific end-state. "Fenced" money is designated to fund the program. The Agency is also directed to keep Congress fully and currently informed regarding the covert action. A very limited group of people are "read in" to the Finding and subsequent reporting based upon the Finding.

Note that CIA does not engage in covert action without Presidential Finding direction. It can collect on topics based upon policymaker needs, but cannot conduct covert actions without such Presidential authorization.

CIA-specific terminology

There are a host of terms used within the Agency (CIA's most common term to self-identify). We will limit this discussion to what you might commonly hear in the hallways or in conversations in conference rooms.

The most important improvement you can make in your writing is calling CIA employees "**intelligence officers**", rather than the more commonly incorrectly-used "agents". In CIA parlance, "agents", also known as "assets" or "sources", are foreign-based HUMINT sources. In most federal agencies, "agent" is used to refer to an employee of that agency; not so for the CIA.

In addition to simply assuming that "all Government employees are alike" and thus should be called "agents", the "CIA agent" terminology might have developed in the early 1950s, when the CIA employed U.S. citizens as "staff Agents" and Contract Agents". Present-day nomenclature is "operations officer."

Employees are federal employees on the General Schedule (**GS**) scale, which ranges from GS-1 to GS-15 officers (in earlier years, the grades reached GS-18, called "supergrades"). Each of these ranks has ten pay steps, which can overlap with other pay grades' steps. These GS grades are rough equivalents to military ranks. A GS-15 is roughly a Colonel; a GS-14 a Lieutenant Colonel; a GS-13 a Major; etc.

When one is promoted above GS-15, one joins the ranks of the Senior Intelligence Service (SIS; a similar Senior Executive Service exists in other federal agencies), equivalent to General officers in the military. These senior officers are referred to as SISrs. At the highest levels of the Agency (D/CIA and DD/CIA) is Executive Pay (EP). Unlike the private sector, where one's pay is treated as a state secret, CIA officers generally know each other's GS grade, although they are not rank-conscious in terms of personal address. Everyone addresses each other by first name (in some cases, they might not actually know one's real last name!), often including the Director.

Employees are evaluated against standards to move from one level to the next, although eventually they are ranked against each other for more senior grades. Employees doing well are deemed "competitive" for promotion.

Individuals without onward assignments are called "**hall walkers**," in search of their next position.

Everyone has a "**hall file**"—one's reputation amongst one's colleagues. Although everyone has formal written performance reviews, the hall file can trump the written file when determining whether you want a specific individual on your team.

Agency employees focus on the "**mission**" of the Agency—providing intelligence to policymakers.

Intelligence officers are usually assigned to a home component, usually a regional or functional division (or office, depending upon the Directorate in which they work). At times, they will take an assignment outside that home office. The typical term for this is being "on rotation". One can be **on rotation** to another office, directorate, or even other federal agency.

In the Washington, D.C. area, one can be assigned to Headquarters, a complex of buildings in Langley, Virginia. There are also "**outbuildings**" that house specific offices, but are still considered part of the Headquarters complex in the eyes of those posted "outside the Beltway" (The Beltway—Route 495—is a high-trafficked superhighway for commuters that surrounds Washington, D.C. Contractors who work for the Intelligence Community are often called "Beltway Bandits".). Operations-focused employees, analysts, and others working on the same regions and topics are physically **collocated** (note spelling) in **Centers**.

When working outside the Headquarters area, one can be assigned to a **Station**, usually in the capital city of a country. **Bases**, usually sited outside the capital city, are smaller facilities reporting to the Station. The senior-most member of the Station is called the Chief of Station (COS, pronounced Cee Oh Ess, usually followed by the name of the capital city. It should never be pronounced as "coss" (rhymes with floss). The senior-most base official is the Chief of Base (COB), again followed by the name of the city. Things get done overseas by resident intelligence officers in stations and bases. Singleton heroes, like James Bond, do not go jet-setting around the globe, individually saving the world and trampling the local equities of the intelligence service's forward-deployed representatives.

When a case officer is going off on a recruitment pitch, colleagues wish him "good hunting".

While most Washington bureaucracies revel in acronyms, you do not need to mimic all of them in your writing. Two are fairly important to establish credibility:

The **PDB** is the *President's Daily Brief* (in some eras, called the *President's Daily Briefing*). Depending upon the administration, it can be delivered as a physical book, orally, or virtually. Its dissemination varies according to the preferences of the incumbent President.

An **SDR** is a Surveillance Detection Route. One engages in SDRs to ensure that the local service, be it intelligence or law enforcement, or hostile organization has not put an officer under surveillance. Engaging in an operational act, such as meeting an asset, while under surveillance raises counterintelligence problems for all involved. Make sure that if you use the term, your characters are using the acronym appropriate for their specialty. SDRs to an economic analyst refer to Special Drawing Rights of the International Monetary Fund. The British Ministry of Defence conducts a Strategic Defense Review. A character can walk out of a conversation believing that one thing was said but an entirely different thing was meant by one's colleagues who were speaking a different dialect of bureaucratese.

Speaking of surveillance SDRs: shoes do not come untied so that you can lean down and turn around to scope out whatever surveillance could be behind you. Do not have your character stop and look both ways before entering or after exiting an entrance or exit. Your characters should not appear to be surveillance-conscious, looking around for surveillance. That's a sure tip-off to the local service that your intelligence officer is an intelligence officer. Similarly, one does not "shake" surveillance by running stoplights and taking corners at high speeds. That ensures even more surveillance.

The Agency has other specialized language—aliases, pseudos, crypts, for example—which are sufficiently arcane as to confuse the reader and divert attention from your story. It is far easier for the writer and the reader to simply avoid attempting to employ these concepts, rather than use them ineptly.

One colleague noted that Agency officers often use foreign phrases. "For example, analysts will have an article 'in train', which means in draft. It derives from the French 'en train'".

CIA has a "char force, but most folks look bewildered when I use that term." It is likely that a member of the char force (the cleaning service) will be nearby in virtually every scene you write about Headquarters.

Common Bureaucratese

Washington bureaucrats speak a dialect of American English that sounds like standard English, but can have different meanings. In addition, the Intelligence Community has its own variants of bureaucratese. Common terms include:

- "This Town" refers to Washington, D.C., as in "that's how things are done in This Town" or "you'll never work in This Town again". This Town usually includes the three branches of government, the news media, research organizations, contracting companies, and the commentariat. It usually does not include academia and firms that do not do business with the government.
- "Downtown" refers to government facilities in Washington, D.C. per se.
- "Customers" are any individuals who use an intelligence product. They are usually policymakers, but sometimes include analysts in other organizations.
- "Beltway Bandits", rarely referred to as "Parkway Patriots", are contracting firms usually doing business with defense and intelligence agencies. The Beltway is a circular highway (route 495) that rings Washington, D.C. The George Washington (GW) Parkway is a commuter road for Northern Virginians (always capitalized, as if NoVa was the 51st state) going to work in downtown D.C.
- ICs. When plural, IC refers to independent contractors, not affiliated with a contracting firm. When singular, IC refers to the Intelligence Community.

- Appropriation, Authorization, and Continuing Resolution are terms referring to how the Intelligence Community, and the federal government at large, is funded. Committees in the House of Representatives and Senate appropriate annual funding for federal agencies. Separate oversight committees in the House and Senate authorize the use of these funds. When the House and Senate cannot agree on an annual overarching federal budget (which happens often), sometimes the houses will adopt a Continuing Resolution, which will fund the federal government for a specified period (usually a few weeks), at the same level of spending as was the case for the previous fiscal year. On occasions in which Congress does not pass a Continuing Resolution, the government technically shuts down and no one can legally be paid. Employees are "on furlough", and usually are paid retroactively (although there are no guarantees). Some employees are designated essential, and can be forced to work without pay.

Intelligence Products

IC agencies with a collection mission refer to their products as "INTs"—types of intelligence. They often are referred to as "raw" intelligence or "unprocessed" intelligence and can include
- **HUMINT:** intelligence coming from human beings (assets/agents/sources)
- **SIGINT:** signals intelligence
- **COMINT:** communications intelligence, a subset of SIGINT
- **ELINT:** electronic intelligence, such as telemetry
- **PHOTINT:** photographic intelligence, generally called imagery
- **MASINT:** measurement and signatures intelligence, derived from tech that samples the air, soil, radiation, water, etc.
- **OSINT:** open source intelligence, such as newspapers, radio/television, the Internet
- **Rumint:** Not an officially-recognized intelligence type, but rumor intelligence has the fastest dissemination time through IC hallways of any of the INTs. It is sometimes called corridor radio.

"Finished Products" are produced by intelligence agencies with an analytical component. Products can be written or oral briefings, short-, medium- or long-term, constituting several pages or shorter than a tweet (originally called "snowflakes" in some forms of daily finished intelligence, not to be confused with the "snowflake" tasking memos issued by then-Secretary of Defense Donald Rumsfeld or the "snowflake" derogative term used for the American political left).

Counterintelligence

Counterintelligence (CI) can also be considered a product of IC organizations. "Little CI" refers to the meticulous process that goes into catching individual spies. "Big CI" refers to determining what targets are of interest to foreign intelligence services and attempting to protect against their attempts to penetrate these targets. In counseling intelligence officers being assigned overseas, CI officers observe that "A 5 getting on the plane is not a 10 getting off the plane. If people way outside your dating league express a sudden interest in your, consider their motivation. You haven't suddenly become more charming." A similar version was offered in the television show *House* by principal character Dr. Gregory House: 3s date 3s, 10s date 10s. Spotting a spy can take years of patient investigation.

Bureaucratic Language Barriers

The slang used within an IC agency is often dependent upon its type of mission and can complicate inter-agency communication. Common terms, particularly nouns and verbs, can lead to misunderstandings across agency lines when idiosyncratic meaning are assigned to those terms. Consider "cover", which means:
- One's official headgear in the armed services
- Providing suppressing fire during a military encounter
- Analyzing a topic by an analyst, who "covers" an "account" such as Russian economics, terrorism in Africa, or leadership in Asia

- the "legend" a covert officer provides about one's reason for being in a country, or in a location, called one's "cover story"

Similarly, "secure the building" means to:

- a security officer: Ensuring the physical, personnel, and cyber security of a facility
- a member of the armed forces in a firefight: ensuring that no hostile personnel remain in the building
- a logistics officer: obtaining a favorable 5-year lease on the facility

The acronym EOD can make for puzzling conversations.

- At CIA, it means Entry on Duty (one's first day on the job).
- In the military, it can mean explosive ordnance demolition.
- Among some pundits, it can mean end of day (currently a fill-in for "in the final analysis").

Intra-Agency communications can be similarly hampered by language differences within an organization. For example, in the FBI, to special agents dealing with organized crime, "Five Families" refers to the five Mafia families of Italian heritage that plagued New York City in the 20th century, including the Bonanno, Colombo, Gambino, Genovese and Lucchese families. To an FBI analyst, however, Five Families refer to specific types of written finished intelligence products, such as intelligence bulletins, intelligence appraisals, situational information reports, Weekly Intelligence Reports, and other specialized products.

Organization

The Agency (referred to by CIA officers as "The Agency", to the annoyance of other members of the IC with "Agency" in their names) includes five directorates and a DCI Area of offices serving Agencywide needs. Before the D/CIAship of John Brennan, the four principal directorates were:

- **Operations,** which collects human source intelligence, conducts covert action at the direction of the President via Presidential Findings, and performs counterintelligence. It recently was called the National Clandestine Service. In the Agency's early history, it was also called the Directorate of Plans. Before that, it was two separate offices. Make sure you use the period-correct term.

- **Analysis,** which houses the analytical cadre of the Agency that is devoted to providing finished intelligence to the policymaking community. The Directorate through its history has also been called the Directorate of Intelligence and the National Foreign Assessment Center. If writing about a period in Agency history, be sure to use the period-specific term.
- **Science and Technology,** which houses the scientists and engineers who provide support to operations and develops technical collection methods.
- **Support,** which provides such services as security, health, logistics, finance, communication, information technology, and other assistance to the other Directorates. Throughout its history, it has also been called the Directorate of Administration. Check to make sure your prose is period-correct.

Then-D/CIA John Brennan created a fifth Directorate, that of Digital Innovation, to handle breakthroughs in cyber issues.

There is no pecking order across the Directorates. Rank is in person, rather than in organization or position.

The DCI Area, often referred to as the 7th Floor (the term also includes the individual Directorate leaders), includes offices of Public Affairs, Congressional Affairs, Human Resources, Protocol, General Counsel, Military Affairs, the Talent Center of Excellence, Equal Employment Opportunity, Information Management, the Office of Inspector General, and the like.

The head of a Directorate is a Director *for* X (e.g. Director for Operations, also called the DDO, the Director of the Directorate of Operations). A Directorate is a Directorate *of* X (e.g., Directorate of Analysis). Directors and Directorates are usually referred to by their acronyms, e.g., the DDO (often called Deputy Director for Operations) and DO (Directorate of Operations).

The Agency is also organized by mission centers, bringing together specialists from the Directorates to work on common issues. They include regionally-based centers as well as those focusing on counterterrorism, counterproliferation, counternarcotics, and counterintelligence.

People

Despite the mystique of the lone, sometimes rogue, hero who visits exotic areas of the globe, shoots hundreds of bad guys without having to change a weapon's magazine, gets the girl, and saves the world single-handedly, Agency officers are normal, middle-class, suburban homeowners with mortgages, families, and hobbies. They complain about traffic, parking, lengthy commutes, student loans, rising costs of living, the foibles of local professional, college, and high school sports teams, and typical concerns of other federal employees. Our spouses tend to know where we work and in general terms what we do. CIA officers do not have a union, although some other members of the IC do.

As a colleague observed, "Real spies actually get severely hurt and even die. I get tired of seeing [spy-fi heroes] getting punched 100 times by a guy who is twice their size or get the full brunt of a blast shockwave and walk away without bruises, loss of hearing, broken or missing limbs. Real IC members get hurt and die." I've had friends die in terrorist and other life events like cancer and car accidents. There's a reason the Memorial Wall exists—we are not invulnerable.

Key Job Titles

In addition to being "intelligence officers", CIA employees self-identify by the type of work they do, usually relating to their directorate affiliation. These functional distinctions between, say, analysts and operations officers, are somewhat blurred in non-U.S. intelligence services, in which operations officers are often called upon to serve analytical functions as well. This specialization is often hailed as one of the strengths of the American system. That said, sometimes analysts can become station chiefs and sometimes operations folk try the analytical side of the house.

Analysts, who work in the Directorate of Analysis, are identified as, inter alia, military analysts, leadership analysts, economic analysts, political analysts, et al., depending upon the type of substantive account they cover. Analysts cover country-specific and regional accounts, as well as cyber, counterterrorism, counterproliferation, counterintelligence threats, intelligence collection, science/technology/weapons, and targeting studies. The analysts write for similar products—*President's Daily Briefs*, other regularly-scheduled daily products, National Intelligence Estimates, and tailored appraisals for specific customers—as well as products unique to their accounts, such as special reports on international terrorism, or situation reports on ongoing crises. Their job is not to make pinpoint predictions on, say, elections ("Candidate A will get 42.58% of the vote in the upcoming Ruritanian election."), but rather serve as a guide through the meaning of all of the incoming data about the election and the implications for U.S. policy on the likeliest outcomes.

In this regard, policymakers abhor nuance but analysts love it, believing as well that just one more piece of information, from whatever source, will improve their understanding of the situation. As a senior manager mentioned to me, analysts' "knowledge is encyclopedic, wide and deep". Some policymakers welcome detail-oriented presentations, but most argue that they do not have the time to devote to long briefings or papers. Analysts understand this need for the big picture, but will happily conduct a "deep dive" (more thoroughgoing look at the details) when encouraged by an audience.

Officers in the Directorate of Operations include:
- **Operations Officers**, who go overseas to spot, assess, develop, recruit, and handle assets
- **Staff Operations Officers**, who provide (usually Headquarters-based) support to the operations of stations and bases
- **Collection Management Officers**, who vet the substantive reporting of clandestine assets and disseminate their reports
- **Targeters**, who assist with identifying potential sources of intelligence
- **Specialists** (terms will differ) including those whose careers are focused on, say, counterintelligence or covert action or conduct paramilitary operations.

- **Language Officers** who have native or near-native fluency in critical languages. Despite what you may see on spy-fi TV shows, not every CIA officer speaks dozens of languages.
- Those in the training program of the Directorate of Operations can include **Professional Trainees** (PTs), who are straight out of college and serve interim assignments on Headquarters desks before beginning their more extensive tradecraft training and Clandestine Service Trainees, who have more life and professional experience than the PTs, and move into their tradecraft training directly after their swearing-in ceremony.

Science and Tech Officers include individuals who design gadgetry used in the field, run research and development programs to provide technology solutions to intelligence problems, and themselves conduct technical operations in the field. Specialties include:

- Biology
- Chemistry
- Computer Science
- Mathematics
- Physics
- Various Engineering Fields, such as:
  - Aerospace
  - Chemical
  - Computer
  - Electrical
  - Mechanical
  - Systems

Admin Officers keep any large organization running, as well as provide CIA-specific services. They have backgrounds in security, logistics, finance, human resources, law, information technology, infrastructure, and medical services.

D/CIA Area Officers provide special services to the "7th Floor"—the senior-most leadership of the Agency—in such fields as public affairs,

Congressional affairs, law, Inspector General oversight, Equal Employment Opportunity, and diversity.

Management Titles

The Agency does not have an extensive hierarchy. In general, the smallest unit is called a branch, which might have less than ten people. It is run by a Branch Chief. A Group Chief will have several Branch Chiefs reporting to him/her. In the Directorate of Operations, a Division Chief will manage several groups. An Office Director is the equivalent in the other Directorates. Each Directorate is run by a Deputy Director. Third in the management hierarchy for the entire Agency is the Chief Operating Officer (previously called the Executive Director). The Director of the Central Intelligence Agency is assisted by a Deputy Director of the CIA.

The overseas management structure is similarly compact. There can be branches, reporting to a Chief of Base or Chief of Station. Base Chiefs report to a Station Chief. COSs and COBs usually have reached their position via other "tours" (jobs) within the Directorate of Operations, but there are instances of successful COSs who grew up in the Directorate of Analysis and reached the highest levels of the Agency.

Self-Identification

Agency officers generally serve overseas in true name (their given name). For operational purposes, they sometimes need to operate in alias, which will have varying degrees of backstopping, depending upon operational needs. One may also be known by one's organizational acronym. For example, the Chief of East Asian Division would be referred to as C/EA.

One is also identified by a badge, worn above the waist. Blue badges are for staff officers. Green badges are for contractors. V badges are assigned to visitors who must be escorted in Agency buildings. Several other badges exist, but you won't need to use them in your writing. Overseas, CIA officers do not wear badges that indicate CIA affiliation. No overseas badges or signage should have the CIA logo.

A VISIT TO CIA HEADQUARTERS

ROUTE 123 ENTRANCE

Erroneous spy-fi television and movies show CIA Headquarters in various locations, sometimes in downtown Washington, D.C., or elsewhere. CIA's Headquarters building is located in Langley, Virginia, just outside residential McLean, Virginia. The main entrance is on Route 123, near the route 193 turnoff. Numerous photos are available from media coverage of the attack on Agency employees on January 25, 1993. There is extensive signage marking the entrance.

Photo provenance Google Earth

GW PARKWAY ENTRANCE SIGN

A second entrance is off the George Washington Parkway.

Photo provenance unknown

HEADQUARTERS

The Headquarters Compound, formally known as the George Bush Center for Intelligence, named after former DCI and President George Herbert Walker Bush, comprises 258 acres, on which one finds the Original (often incorrectly termed "Old") and New Headquarters Buildings and several secondary buildings. On the other side of the fence is the Federal Highway Administration building. Headquarters is surrounded by woodlands. You can see the Potomac River from the topmost floors.

Alamy Stock Photo

The entrance to the Original Headquarters Building has a distinctive awning. As one approaches it, you'll find a 500-seat auditorium, colloquially called The Bubble. Just behind it is a Memorial Pond, dedicated to those who gave their lives to the Agency's mission.

WMAL photo, taken before the new addition was built.
Arrow points to The Bubble auditorium

FINDING PARKING

After going through processing at security gates, one then engages in a time-worn ritual at Headquarters, finding parking. The lots, previously referred to by their geographic locations (e.g., West Lot, North Lot, etc.) are now designated by colors. There is also a three-tier parking deck. Some of the spots are reserved for senior officers, those with handicaps, and carpoolers. Elevators in Headquarters also have color designations. A very few very senior officers have designated spots in a senior garage; your characters will never park there. There is no parking immediately against the building.

Photo from Courthousenews.com

Cool Stuff to See While Finding Parking:

Soviet Mi-17 helicopter

This Soviet-made helicopter was used in the Afghan war. It arrived at CIA's Headquarters compound in 2018; make sure you don't inadvertently write an anachronism.

Photo from thedrive.com

A-12 Oxcart

Commonly misrepresented as an SR-71 (which is the Air Force nomenclature), the CIA's plane is more correctly called the A-12 Oxcart. The plane was installed in the Headquarters compound during the leadership of D/CIA Michael Hayden. Again, be careful of anachronism.

The Oxcart is located across from the parking deck, next to what was called West Lot.

Photo from CIA.gov

Photo from CIA.gov

Photo from CIA.gov

WELCOME TO NHB

The New Headquarters Building's entrance is a short walk from the parking deck.

Photo from CIA.gov

INSIDE THE BUBBLE

The distinctive dome of the auditorium features a series of different-sized circles. There is a small stage at the front and a projection booth in the rear.

Photo from CIA.gov

NATHAN HALE STATUE

A statue of Nathan Hale, a Revolutionary War operations officer who was captured and hanged by the British, stands a few yards from the Memorial Pond. The same statue also graces the grounds of Yale University and Phillips Academy in Andover, Massachusetts, Hale's (and former President George H.W. Bush's) college and prep school, respectively. the Hale statue is a permanent reminder of the importance of careful tradecraft. Officers sometimes leave change at Hale's feet.

Photo by Cynthia Kwitchoff

MEMORIAL GARDEN/KOI POND

The Memorial Garden and Koi Pond offer a quiet place for Agency officers to reflect on the sacrifices by their colleagues over the years.

Photo from CIA.gov

9/11 MEMORIAL

A beam from the World Trade Center stands in tribute to those who died in the al-Qaeda attacks.

Photo from CIA.gov

THE BERLIN WALL FRAGMENT

A graffiti'd portion of the Berlin Wall greets employees walking to a side entrance of Original Headquarters Building from a parking lot.

Photo from CIA.gov

WELCOME TO OHB

This is the view of the OHB entrance from the Bubble. While it is a photogenic entrance, most employees use other entranceways.

Photos from CIA.gov

THE AGENCY SEAL IN THE OHB LOBBY

As one walks through the glass doors, one immediately sees the Agency Seal, featuring a compass rose that symbolizes the Agency's coverage of world events.

THE MEMORIAL WALL

On your right, just past the Seal, is the Memorial Wall. A star is etched for every Agency staff employee who died while in service to our country. It is flanked by the American flag and the Agency flag. As of March 2019, there are 133 stars. Virtually everyone in the Agency knew someone represented by a star. There are numerous photos of the Memorial Wall across the Internet. Try to get this one correct. It's sacred to Agency officers.

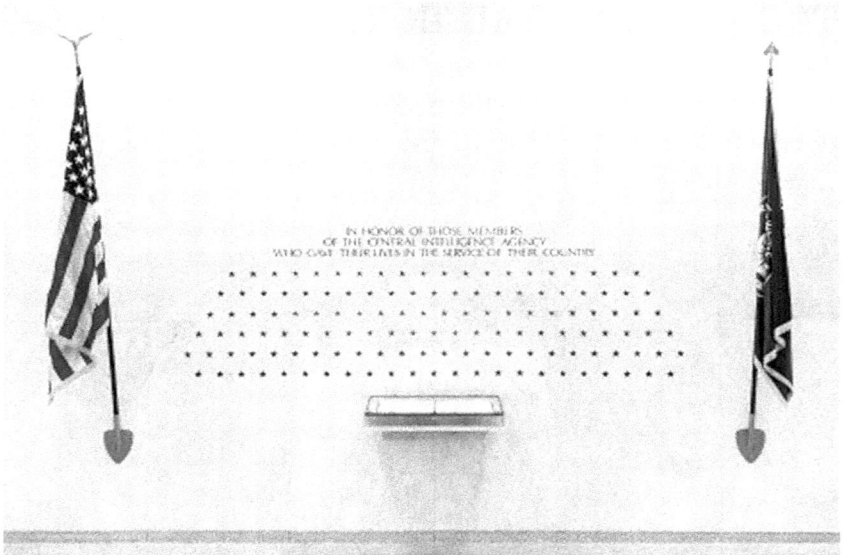

Photo from CIA.gov

The Book of Honor

Just beneath the constellation of stars is the Book of Honor, listing the dates America's heroes fell, as well as their names. Some of the names are not listed; even in death, their covers (and by extension, their names, assets, and operations) must be protected.

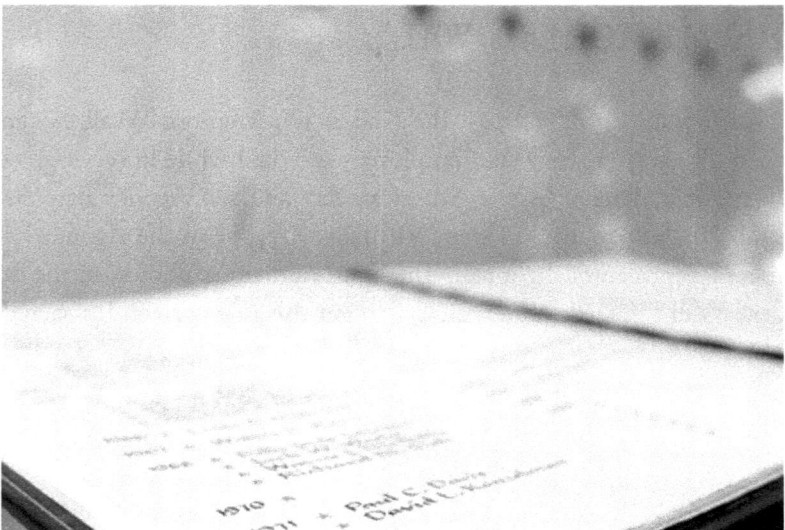

Photo from CIA.gov

THE DONOVAN STATUE AND OSS MEMORIAL WALL

On the facing wall is a similar Book of Honor for the Office of Strategic Services (OSS) officers who died serving America in World War II. Only one star symbolizes their ultimate sacrifice. The book is flanked by the U.S. flag and a statue of William J. Donovan, the only Director of the OSS.

Photo from CIA.gov

The OSS Book of Honor

The book lists the name of the OSS officers who died serving our country.

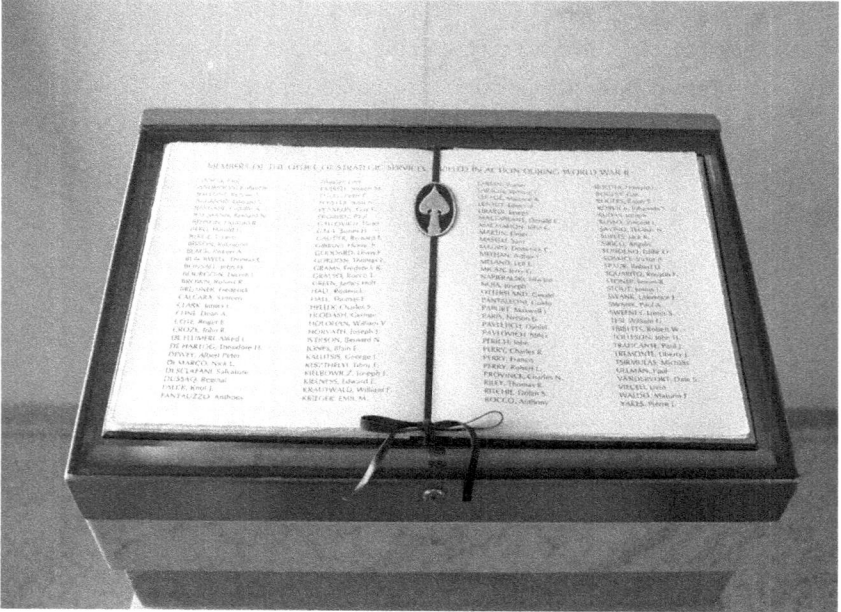

Photo from CIA.gov

CIA'S MOTTO

Also on the OSS wall is a Biblical passage on the centrality of seeking the truth.

Photo from CIA.gov

TOP OF THE STAIRS:
THE GEORGE H.W. BUSH BUST

After passing through another level of security and walking up the stairs, one arrives at a bust of former DCI and President George H. W. Bush, flanked by the U.S. and CIA flags. Behind the bust is a small court-yard.

Photo from CIA.gov

PRESIDENTIAL PORTRAIT GALLERY:
P41 AND P43

The first floor of OHB features several exhibits, including portraits, with signed notes from each President who has been served by CIA. Note the similarities of the signatures of President George H.W. Bush and his son, President George W. Bush.

To the CIA, an indispensable agency, -- especially the men and women who serve with dedication - distinction

Gg Bush

To the men and women of the CIA - Our nation is stronger and safer thank to your dedication and hard work Ggo Bh

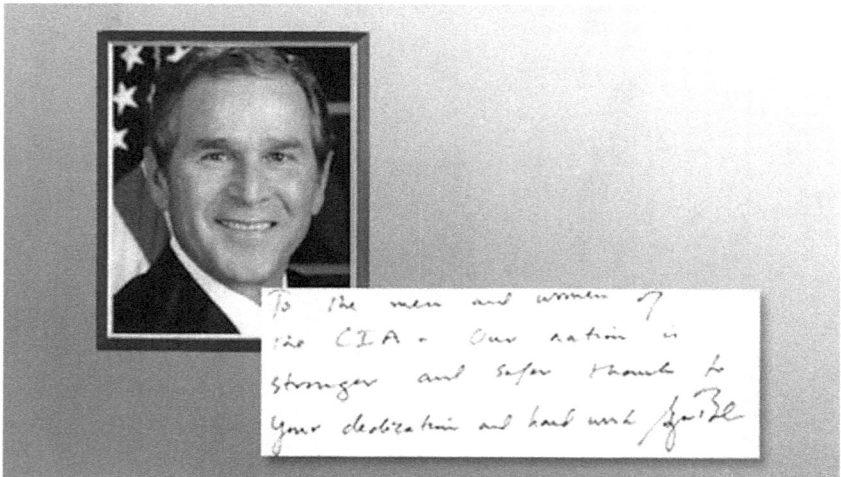

Photos from CIA.gov

THE DCI PORTRAIT GALLERY

On a corridor perpendicular to the Bush bust corridor one finds the DCI Portrait Gallery, which, since D/CIA Porter Goss, also includes the newly-named D/CIAs. The portraits include cards which detail the years served by each Director. Portraits generally are painted after a Director steps down.

Photo from CIA.gov

MELZAC COLLECTION: WASHINGTON COLOR SCHOOL

Throughout OHB and NHB, one will find exemplars of the Washington Color School, a form of non-objective/non-representational art that explored ways to use large solid areas of paint, developed by six core abstract expressionist artists during the 1950s–1970s.

Photo from CIA.gov

REPRESENTATIONAL ARTWORK

More recently, the halls of the Headquarters buildings have been decorated by more representational pieces depicting activities relevant to the mission of the Agency. Other floors of the Agency include photos and ephemera relevant to the particular Offices and Divisions that are housed there.

Photo from CIA.gov. "First Sting" Stuart Brown/Oil on Canvas, 2008/ Donated Courtesy of Richard J. Guggenhime and Donald Elster

DA MUSEUM ARTIFACTS

CIA's museum staff has curated thousands of items from CIA history, displaying them in hallways dedicated to various Directorates. This one shows the history of analytic work.

Photo from CIA.gov

DS&T MUSEUM ARTIFACTS

Some of the small technical gadgetry used in-person and/or at a distance are featured in the DS&T hallway.

Photo from CIA.gov

Robofish

Particularly popular among visitors to the DS&T hallway is a robotic fish, which mimicked the movements of a catfish, but had sensors that could collect critical intelligence.

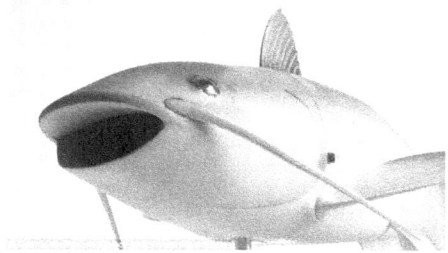

Photos from CIA.gov

Insectothopter

Near the robofish is an insectothopter, built in the 1970s, which is roughly the size of a dragonfly, and also equipped with intelligence-collecting sensors. It is the intellectual ancestor of intelligence collection drones.

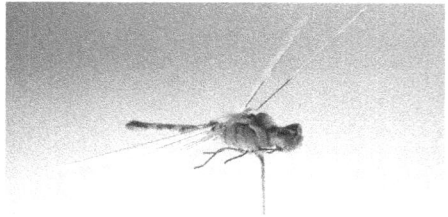

MAIN OHB MUSEUM ENTRANCE

The Main OHB Museum often changes the displays, which usually depict the work of operations officers.

Photo from CIA.gov

Bin Laden's AK-47

An eye-catching artifact is Osama bin Laden's personal weapon.

The 2-3 Person Submersible

On the other side of an OHB elevator is a small submersible, which could move into shallow waters undetected.

Photos from CIA.gov

THE HEADQUARTERS CAFETERIA

Yes, CIA has a Starbucks; no names on the cups, though. There are other familiar fast food vendors as well.

THE MAIN LIBRARY

Not all useful material comes from cables. The Agency's librarians often help analysts and others find that useful piece of information from publicly available (open) sources.

Photos from CIA.gov

WTC FLAG

A flag that flew over the World Trade Center.

Photo from CIA.gov

KRYPTOS SCULPTURE, OHB-NHB COURTYARD

Artist James Sanborn created a four-piece set of sculptures that feature a series of coded messages. The main sculpture was dedicated on November 3, 1990. It resides in the courtyard between OHB and NHB, outside the cafeteria.

Photo from CIA.gov

BEFORE COMPUTERS, THERE WAS...

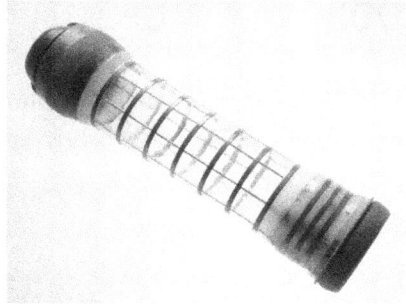

A series of pneumatic tubes, similar to what are used in drive-through banks, were used to quickly move messages between floors of OHB.

Photo from CIA.gov

NHB OVERHEAD MUSEUM

Large models of Agency overhead collection planes, including an Oxcart, a U-2, and a small drone, patrol the skies of the NHB Atrium.

Photos from CIA.gov

DONOVAN MUSEUM

Dedicated to William Donovan, Director of the Office of Strategic Services (OSS) during World War II. OSS was the precursor to the CIA.

Photo from CIA.gov

THE GYM

NHB and OHB each have workout rooms. Many employees also enjoy running on the grounds. Each year a 5K run is held. Former D/CIA David Petraeus ran six miles per day, often listening to briefings by analysts who ran with him. D/CIA Hayden was also seen running around the compound's perimeter.

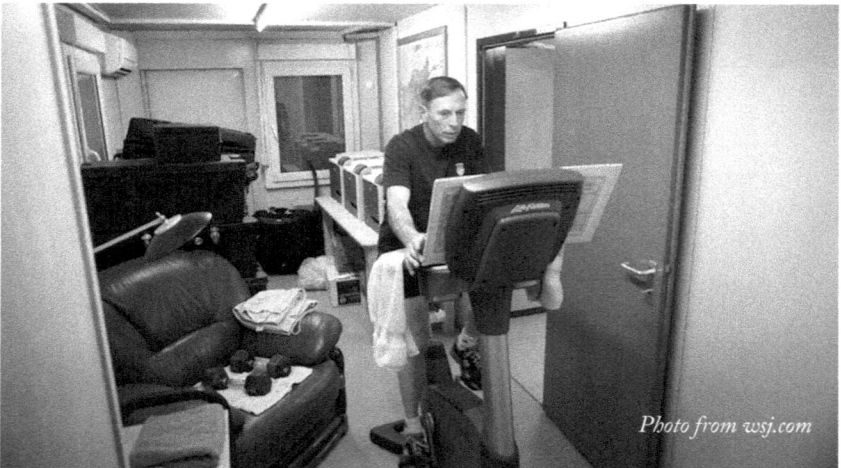

Photo from wsj.com

DIRECTOR'S CONFERENCE ROOM

The D/CIA's conference room is immediately outside the Director's office on the 7th floor of OHB. The senior management of the Agency is often referred to as the 7th Floor.

Photo from nbcnews.com

EVERY DESK HAS THESE: BURN BAGS

The art director looking to dress up spy-fi intelligence officers' offices/cubicles should start with proper burn bags. When full, employees staple them at the top and throw them into burn chutes.

Desks often have maps, photos, Cabinet organization charts, souvenirs and flags from relevant countries. Some analysts keep an emergency suit and tie for those times when they are not expecting to be called downtown to brief during Casual Friday.

Each desk has a secure and a non-secure phone; both are land lines. No cell phones are permitted. One cannot magically say "go secure" on a non-secure phone.

Offices as a whole are also festooned with rows of conserva-files, despite the Digital Revolution. Desks rarely have physical in-boxes, but paper still exists, with Post-It notes and phone message slips being very popular.

Every day, somewhere in Headquarters, there will be construction going on as offices are reconfigured due to the latest reorganization or creation of a new task force to respond (the IC term is "surge") to the latest crisis. The construction projects' detritus can be seen in the hallways as well as the office spaces.

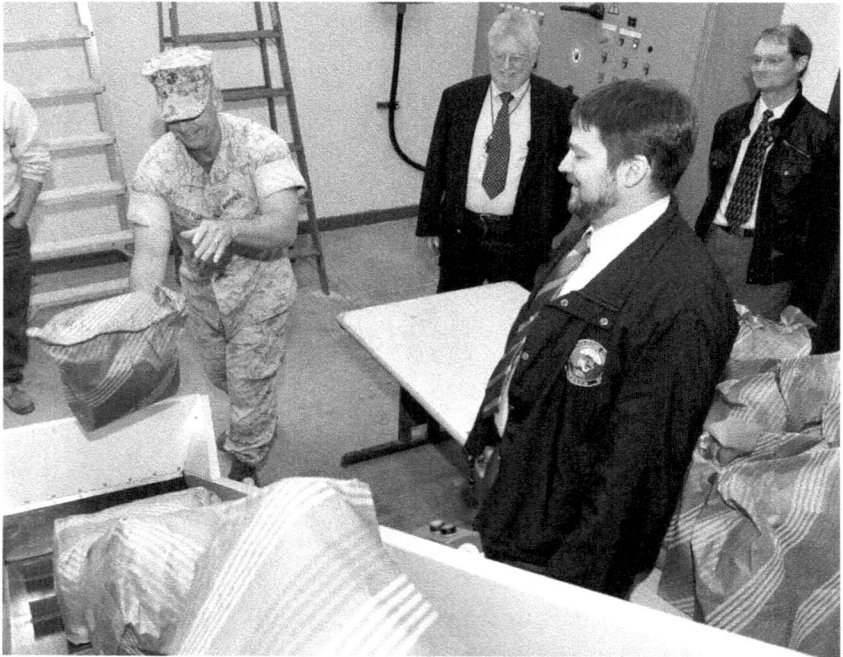

Public domain photo by Staff Sgt. Javier Cruz, as published in https://www. airforcemedicine.af.mil/News/Photos/igphoto/2000370073/ courtesy of Air Force Surgeon General's Office of Public Affairs

EVERY DESK HAS THIS: INTELLIPEDIA

The Intelligence Community's equivalent of Wikipedia allows officers across the Community to share observations about ongoing events and topics of critical concern to policymakers.

Wikipedia

EVERY DESK HAS THIS: INTELINK

Officers also rely upon the Intelink system for cross-agency communication.

Desktops usually have open a copy of a word processing program and a feed of the day's cable traffic (messages from embassies, intercepted communications, human source reports, and the like).

Despite what you've seen on TV, one cannot meander over to a colleague's workstation, defeat the encryption, and log into any system in the world with three keystrokes. However, computer systems don't always work properly, and sometimes the frustrations that you've experienced with your own system will be articulated by intelligence officers.

Photo from intelink.gov

EVERY DESK

CIA's first Instagram photo

DON'T FORGET TO VISIT THE GIFT SHOP

One of the most popular sites on the first floor of OHB is the Employee Activities Association (EAA) store. If it exists, you can put a CIA logo on it. Someone probably has.

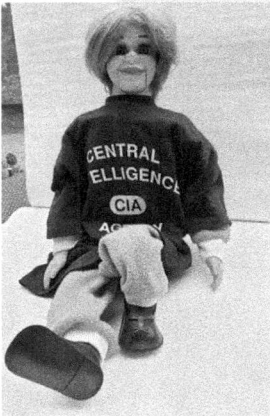

Photos courtesy of Susan Schjelderup; ventri-lo-American courtesy of Dr. Ciana Mickolus

This walk-through Headquarters should help you give your audience a flavor of the physical facility in which your characters operate.

// ⊕ //

COMMON ERRORS
AND HOW TO AVOID THEM

In preparing this book, I polled several hundred Intelligence Community colleagues, both alumni and serving officers, on what they would recommend to authors regarding how to more accurately portray the intelligence business. Here are a few of their insights, sometimes directly quoted to give you a feeling for how we express ourselves, sometimes paraphrased.

Several colleagues mentioned commonly-held myths about our work, including that CIA:

- spies on US citizens
- operates independently and is not held accountable to anyone
- careers will earn you fame and recognition
- makes foreign policy
- officers are the keepers of all government secrets

These myths were sufficiently laid to rest in our discussion of the Agency's mission and the roles of its employees, but it's helpful to recount them here as a reminder.

Many books and movies "make most intelligence work out to be more glamorous, exciting, dangerous, and romantic than in real life." Even when it is exciting, sometimes Hollywood can overdo it, or expect too much. I once had a real-life story of a CIA team that foiled Cubans from setting off explosives in a prison of counterrevolutionaries turned down because it lacked sex.

Common threads for successful real-life operations officers are the ability to deal with ambiguity, patience, and maintaining focus. "Most novels and Hollywood portrayals have everything coming together with lots of action and no down time. While decisions on the fly are occasionally needed, more often we would try to think through a task first, even talking it over with an experienced colleague."

- "In the first instance one never has all the information needed. This is when experience and your 'gut feeling' come into play.
- "One also needs patience in seeing an operational task through. Some operations can take more than a year. Patience also comes to bear when running counter surveillance before a meeting or operational task.
- "While waiting for a few details to be acquired or fall into place, maintaining focus is paramount. This is also true on long surveillance."

Superhero-Class Athletic/Military Skills

"Hollywood has us skilled in Special Forces/SEAL training and maintenance of the physical shape needed for those skills. Some of us had that training in previous military stints and maintained ourselves but most did not."

In addition, we are "not qualified to drive, fly, or sail any vehicle we come across. No, you can't jump into an enemy tank and take off to rescue the girl. Likewise, the average spy can't disarm a bomb without blowing themselves up."

Everyone has their own specialties, and they are called in to operations when needed. One does not try to develop skills on-the-fly while on an operation.

"Instead of typically canonizing the tall, handsome, male case officer, they ought to realize that some of the greatest ops have been run by quiet, retiring, bald guys who are non-threatening and, better yet, low profile. Female officers with little beyond 'wife cover' who can wander about in third world souks without attracting any surveillance or even much attention can often do stuff their high-profile husbands would never be able to pull off." Stated more wryly, another colleague observed, "They also portray us as much better-looking than we really are."

In addition, writers often portray "operations officers as loners, womanizing, and quick on the trigger. Most are family men and women. The best of us behave if for no other reason than operational security. Families are very important to the regular work of an ops officer. They are often used to make contact with and develop targets. One's children may be in the same school as the target's children. Wives socialize together."

As we often tell our new employees, James Bond (or other fill-in-the-blank spy-fi character) would not last five minutes in the real world of espionage. He is simply too high profile. As a colleague counselled, "the essence of clandestinity is that you are not detected. Real life spying is in many ways boring. We don't regularly go around shooting our way out of trouble." We do not get into trouble at the start. We carefully work on not being noticed. "The way action stars crash around what we consider denied areas is total fantasy. The local services own the place, and you are lucky to work between the raindrops very carefully, slowly, and not too often." Moreover, "one person is never at the center of all the action. It takes tens if not hundreds of people, both in the field and at home, to conduct a good operation. But readers (and viewers) want to focus on one person they can admire."

Genius-Level Linguistic Skills

Similarly, Hollywood revels in depicting multi-lingual operations officers who routinely spout off flawless idiomatic Russian, Mandarin, Arabic, and Farsi, sometimes all in the same meeting. Language acquisition, while treasured at the Agency, takes time. One can spend years getting to even "kitchen fluency" in a hard language.

Putting the band back together because current staff lacks their skills

Spy-fi stories often look to reactivating retired former Agency officers, analysts, tech wizards, law enforcement officers or random other government employees who are called upon to support a highly sensitive operation. These alumni "read in" to complex cases in three minutes, then rush off, often by themselves, to save the world. While some retirees come back on contract to their bureaucratic alma maters, or sometimes to related agencies, it is usually in a training or "historic lessons learned" capacity. Similarly, spy-fi writers often show Agency officers pulling old sources out of a hat as a solution for a complex problem. This rarely happens. There's a reason why an asset's relation with the Agency was terminated; usually it's erosion of their access to sensitive information. Once we retire, we don't have access to classified information. Once assets are retired, they don't have access, either.

Going Rogue

Novelists and screenwriters often embrace the myth of the rogue operations officer, or rogue operation, or an entire Agency that has gone rogue. "The villain of convenience is generally the CIA, usually in a plot to overthrow the U.S. government." (Or it's the FBI as part of the mythical "deep state", if conspiracy theorists are to be believed.) A rogue "agent" (sic) in spy-fi quickly becomes the celebrated American rugged individualist fighting "the system", a "government gone bad", or a pernicious cabal within the very fabric of government. Some rogue agencies are depicted as protecting the American way of life, others as pursuing more nefarious goals. None of that happens in real life. Individuals within the Agency have a strong sense of individual accountability, and the Agency as a whole has a complex system for monitoring and reporting activities. This extends to protecting against unintentional introduction of bias in analytic methods as well as oversight of collection and covert action operations.

Spy-fi singleton rogue "agents" (sic) are sometimes portrayed as willing to take on the system with which one agrees, but is simply too bureaucratically ossified to do the right thing in a timely fashion. The individualist then takes it upon himself to show initiative and not wait for the dithering Headquarters to get its act together. Such unauthorized actions by loose cannons, sometimes called "cowboys", are quickly reined in in the real world, if they ever get started.

Conspiracies

Some spy-fi writers have the Agency engage in plots with evil Washington cabals, assuming that everyone in intelligence has conservative political leanings. While Agency officers vote, political leanings rarely come up in corridor conversations. One sometimes knows the political leanings of a Director by reading their bio, but once in the Agency, we serve the policymaker, whatever their party affiliation.

Contrary to the beliefs of conspiracy theorists, there is no other really, really undercover CIA that uses "Langley CIA" as a distraction. We're the only CIA, no matter how inconvenient that may be to your proposed plot.

By the way, the CIA was not involved in the JFK assassination, Elvis is not a CIA staffer, and there are no UFOs or extraterrestrials in the CIA's Headquarters buildings' basements.

There is no such thing as the "deep state." Some IC alumni have criticized the Administration; no one serving has. A former DDO mentioned to me that in much spy fiction, "one of the dark shadowy figures behind most of the dastardly conspiracies to circumvent U.S. law is the DDO—if only they knew!" Agency officers serve whomever is the incumbent President.

A colleague observed, "the larger the group planning something, the more chance there is for it to leak. The giant plot involving a few hundred people isn't likely to remain secret." This also affects operations overseas, and why the need-to-know principle developed.

Some spy-fi writers assume that four or so people are running the CIA and just a few more are running the country. While this would limit the likelihood of leaks, it doesn't bode well for actually getting anything done in an organization the size of the U.S. Government, or even the much smaller Agency.

Rather than attribute an organization's actions to a conspiracy, it is far more likely in the real world that bureaucratic politics—the jockeying within and between agencies—is at work in how groups behave.

As for how organizations behave, operations officers often keep in mind the *"Washington Post* Test"—how would the American public perceive the wisdom of the proposed operation if it appeared on the front page of the *Washington Post*, or *New York Times*, or other major media outlet? Congressional oversight contributes to careful consideration of all aspects of proposals; concern for American sensibilities adds to this. Is this proposal reasonable, and is it consistent with American values? One rarely sees this meticulous weighing of options in spy-fi.

Despite the degree of oversight regarding the IC, your characters should not cite or refer to intelligence-related policies/regulations off the top of their heads as if every intelligence officer/USG official knows every regulation/law by U.S. Code number or formal name. That's why there are separate offices of General Counsel.

Amorality and Moral Equivalence

A colleague noted, "CIA operations officers are often portrayed as being amoral and/or not adhering to any moral code in conducting our work. We are also sometimes portrayed as assassins. While there have been a few instances in the distant past where CIA might have been involved in assassinations, we always operate under the then applicable rules and regulations of the United States Government. CIA attorneys are becoming increasingly more involved in monitoring and in some cases, guiding, every phase of our operations."

Equating CIA activities with, say, those of the erstwhile KGB and its successor organizations is to misunderstand their missions and methods.

The Right Word

Terminology is often misused and misheard by novelists. Moreover, while you want to get it right, too much jargon can also be counterproductive. Among the most frequent errors:

- Remember that "agent" versus "intelligence officer" distinction. And "operatives" is lazy writing.
- We don't call it "Langley". It's "Headquarters".
- Long ago, the Agency was called "The Company". I heard one person refer to it by this moniker in the 43 years of my association as a staffer and contractor. Your characters should not use this anachronism. The term is derived from the Latin American equivalent of LLC or Inc.: cia.
- Similarly, long ago, the Agency, particularly its analytic component, was called the "Pickle Factory". Before the PDB, there was the President's Intelligence Checklist (PICL), pronounced "pickle".
- "I consistently hear 'plausible deniability' but I only remember the use of 'plausible denial.'" The term is more often used regarding covert action rather than collection.

Mission Conflation

Intelligence is not law enforcement. The only members of the Intelligence Community who have law enforcement roles are the FBI, DEA, Coast Guard, and some military counterintelligence investigators. CIA, NSA, DIA, et al., do not have arrest powers.

- One frequently hears recent college graduates say, "I'm thinking of working for CIA, FBI, or other law enforcement agencies." Despite its reporting and analysis sometimes informing law enforcement officers, CIA is not itself a law enforcement agency.
- The National Security Agency is often incorrectly portrayed in spy-fi as having a law enforcement function, spying on virtually every American, or even every person in the world.

- In like manner, "NSA is portrayed as having operators with guns who run operations overseas, who can take over operations from CIA or law enforcement because they are NSA."
- Paramilitary forces are not constantly on alert in every Washington, D.C. office building.
- "The CIA is portrayed as being able to push federal law enforcement around and take over people or cases from them." This just does not happen.
- "State is often portrayed as being able to move in and take over a case or situation; it would never work like that."
- One often sees fictional government officials with authorities that make no sense, such as the Secretary of State having the authority to initiate military or intelligence operations.
- "I've noted the military pushing the FBI around without blowback. I was a military police officer at Ft. Benning and while we always handled military cases, if anything even faintly touched on FBI jurisdiction we immediately notified the FBI and invited them to take over."

This litany of errors reflects common misunderstandings of the missions, roles, and motivations of the various organizations. "Overall, books, movies and TV shows have no idea of the relations among Intelligence Community agencies and between law enforcement and intelligence agencies. There is almost always conflict rather than careful respect for jurisdiction."

A senior officer noted that his main pet peeve about spy-fi "is CIA operating domestically… conducting raids, following targets, etc., all the activities CIA is prohibited from doing by law but somehow always winds up in books and movies… Dramatic, to be sure, but I find it's one of the main misunderstandings of the average citizens whom I talk to or who ask me questions at lectures."

In like manner, while the Office of the Director of National Intelligence strives to facilitate intelligence integration, writers tend to go overboard, with characters alluding to knowledge of secret operations when there is no way another agency/department would have that knowledge. Audiences often are treated to discussions of details/names of Agency officers/assets when there is no way that unit or non-CIA agency would have access to that information.

Immunity

"Any and all foreign embassy personnel are presented as having total diplomatic immunity and have to be immediately released even if they have committed a felony. Not everyone in an embassy has diplomatic immunity, and no one is just released if having committed a felony, and anyone can be held until a ruling from on high is issued." The immunity extends to one's official duties, not ill-considered whims fueled by alcohol.

Communication

Secure communication practice is often poorly portrayed in spy-fi. Agency officers do not wander the corridors and offices with cell phones and personal data assistants. These items can easily be hacked, and are therefore not allowed in any CIA building. Officers do not conduct classified conversations in the hallways, the cafeteria, or restaurants. Officers do not discuss classified material over non-secure phone connections, such as cell phones.

Guns, Guns, Guns

Agency officers do not routinely carry guns, conduct assassinations, or engage in gun battles, car chases, or break-ins. If one is working in a war zone, one might be issued a firearm for personal protection. One does not carry weapons in Headquarters or outbuildings. One does not wear a catsuit and dangle from wires, suspended from the ceiling. Few of us are proficient in martial arts.

Attention to detail in costuming and props can pay off in terms of street cred amongst intelligence professionals.

Gadgets, Gadgets, Gadgets

Agency officers do not drive, need, or want ultra-expensive super-cars that have been heavily gadgeted. Such vehicles attract too much attention by casual observers, not to mention the local intelligence service and police patrols. The nearest Aston Martin DB-5 is in the International Spy Museum in downtown D.C. As one colleague observed, "Spywork is generally slow moving with brief moments of high intensity, not constant action, high speed chases, rogue officers, ad nauseum." Spy-fi treatments often "suffer under the weight of needing to be "Hollywoodized", i.e. always being exciting with everyone getting laid, killed, maimed, or double-crossed, often all at the same time."

"Authors too often conjure fantastic and largely unrealistic capabilities that make communicating with hard-target sources seem like a walk in the park." (While any operation requires careful tradecraft, the "hard targets"—individuals in countries or organizations that are particularly difficult to penetrate, or even get glancing access to—present especially wicked problems.)

Technical capabilities way beyond the state of the science are often shown as routine in spy-fi. One cannot hack into computer systems within three seconds. One cannot crack complex codes in four seconds. Computer display technology is nowhere near as Star Trek-sophisticated as often shown on the big or small screen. As one technically-sophisticated colleague observed, "the most egregious mistakes are regarding technology. We are not nearly as advanced as many novels portray us to be (but it sure would be nice if we actually had what they say we have). Authors should be encouraged to seek out those in the know. Most of us are happy to oblige with no attribution (maybe a signed book!)."

The Opposition is Not Monolithic

"Please show more adequate respect for the capabilities, intelligence, and inventiveness of hostile counterintelligence, Russians, Chinese, Cubans, Iranians, and (historically) the east Europeans, East Germans in particular. Authors should fit the level of tradecraft to the level of hostility of the counterintelligence environment, reserving the top stuff for the most denied areas." Services working for countries other than the above litany are also much more sophisticated than how they are portrayed in spy-fi. Recruiting, or even getting limited access to, hard target individuals is not accomplished by a one-time meeting over cocktails and passing the would-be asset a few bucks under the table.

Saving the World, By Yourself

That said, "in many cases the scale and scope of a story is so much hyperbole. Many great cases in intelligence collection involved a single operations officer and a single source meeting in an out-of-the-way hotel room. The movies with hundreds of people operating in a third country on a covert action that saves the world are very unrealistic."

Much of spy-fi has the main character ignore alarm bells, or not properly plan out an operation. This trait can be traced all the way to the foundation of the Republic, when Nathan Hale was sent out to the field with a paper-thin cover story and no backstopping. Spy-fi heroes still run toward the sound of, well, whatever it is. Brand-new officers, as well as seasoned veterans, are never sent into the field alone. Keep in mind that intelligence is a team effort.

The Flawed Officer

In some popular spy-fi stories, "Out of control head cases are star analysts and operatives". This can extend to actual head cases (psychologists would object to this non-technical diagnosis, but you get the point). The Office of Medical Services would work with these individuals, but would not clear them for the field or other sensitive assignments until the problem had been handled.

Intelligence officers are often shown over-imbibing. As one colleague observes, "one of the things that really bothers me is the apparent medication and alcohol abuse that appears regularly on TV shows about ops officers. The Agency takes seriously the health of its employees. I regularly consulted with the Employee Assistance Program when I suspected employees were in trouble. Analysts need to be 'with it' to write good intelligence."

In many spy-fi stories, opponents are wronged fathers avenging the death of their five-year-old son. While it is considered in some circles fine writing to make the characters multidimensional and sympathetic by making the opponents not all "dark" and the good guys not all "light", "the truth of the matter is that ISIS, al-Qaeda, the Soviet Union, or Mao's China were not nice people."

Be sure to include some inkling that we have a sense of humor, as exemplified by a one-liner sent by a colleague, "My main beef about my tenure in Langley is, I never could tell when I had run out of invisible ink." You might also try to reflect the demographic diversity of the Intelligence Community. CIA is not an Ivy League alumni club of rich white males.

Getting the Era Correct

Be careful of anachronisms.
- O'Toole's, a popular CIA watering hole in nearby McLean, Virginia, shut down several years ago. Do not use it in current-day spy-fi.
- CIA's Rendezvous Room, a cafeteria in the Original Headquarters Building used by covert employees, was repurposed as the Events and Awards Suite years ago.
- Operations Officers are no longer called Case Officers.
- It's D/CIA, not DCI.

Getting the Location Correct

While it's cheaper to film outside Washington, D.C., make sure to get some of the simple locational details right. The subway system, most of it above ground, is called "Metro", not "the subway". There is no Metro stop in Georgetown, or at any of the agencies.

Similarly, be sure to research the foreign locales and correctly describe the sites and local mores and personal habits of foreigners.

COMMON ERRORS AND HOW TO AVOID THEM ■ 91

Getting the Timing Correct

The pacing of spy-fi stories is too time-condensed to ever approach realism. While this is fine for an audience expecting fast-paced action, "events and information should unfold a bit more naturally, using a lot of complex information over a period of time rather than all from a few sources. Consider using 'flashback' more often to bring in new information rather than making it look like things happen/surface within a matter of days or weeks."

Additionally, not everything that happens in an operations officer's day is devoted to specific cases. One spends hours of nonoperational activity establishing, enhancing, and protecting cover and misleading surveillance.

Classification and Clearances

Try to get the simple things, such as cover sheets, correct. There are numerous images of them available on the Internet. Similarly, try to get the classification of a particular document correct. Unclassified, For Official Use Only, Confidential, Secret, Top Secret. Period. Thrilling though it may seem, there is no "above Top Secret", just different accesses (sometimes called "controls") within a compartment, and not everything that your hero(es) are working on is Top Secret. A cover sheet should not say "Classified". The degrees of classifications have different handling requirements.

"Arguing that too many people have clearances is nonsense; it is the access that is important. Clearances with a full background investigation are a positive toward security, not a negative."

Speaking of obtaining clearances, not all federal agencies use polygraphs and background investigations. CIA does. Professionally-conducted polygraph interviews do not use open-ended questions. The answers need to be yes/no. By the way, polygraphs should not be viewed as "lie detectors". They are measuring physical responses, which sometimes might indicate deception.

Plausibility in Plotting

The Director (or Deputy Director) of the CIA, or of any large intelligence organization, should not be portrayed as an active participant, vice a general overseer, in operations. There are simply too many operations ongoing for a D/CIA to become intimately involved. A D/CIA is too high-profile to be seen meeting with an asset. The D/CIA has too many other demands on his/her time to be dealing directly with an operation and/or asset(s).

Moreover, as a colleague observes, "people need to act in a way that reasonably fits their training and status. Occasionally a junior analyst might brief the president, but not as a matter of course. Maybe a general might be clueless, random, evil, or completely incompetent, but then there's got to be some explanation for how he got to that rank through all the filters. An insane D/CIA or operations officer can happen, but how have they avoided the Office of Medical Services (OMS) and reports from their colleagues? There needs to be some recognition that a person's place shapes their options. They can break out of that, but there needs to be an internal logic to the scenario."

Looking just in terms of the craft of writing—and this can be said of any genre of fiction, not just spy fi—"I think my main objection was… the very shallow portrayals of the intelligence officers. There was no depth in creating their characters." People are complex; your characters should be, too.

One senior colleague observes that flaws in plotting might just be inherent in the preferences of fans of the genre. "I suppose the errors I see are less of trade craft (not sure I want all those to be fixed), but more associated with the storytelling. The ideal spy thriller is like a World War II movie - the entire conflict is somehow captured in the actions of a single man or unit in the midst of the maelstrom. That which we find humorous is probably essential to a novel's ability to win a reader's attention. IC days are long, and include a fair amount of bureaucracy and process, no one is ever associated with just one case. Corruption and secret plots wouldn't survive five minutes given the overlapping organizational structures and process oversight. It isn't uncommon for husbands and wives to work in an organization, but very rarely on the same issue. Team work is important but intra-organization competition and alternative simultaneous approaches are not rare. Foreign and domestic adversaries are rarely black and white. Violence is rare, sex among co-workers even rarer, martial arts skills non-existent. We don't use personal telephones in the building, don't need to fly to multiple foreign capitals to work on a case but if we do, it's coach class. We don't abuse or burn through sources and we don't meet at mosques in the middle of Beirut right after prayer time."

So is it safe to write anything without some complaining by the pros? Here's one bit of positive reinforcement from a former senior Agency officer who has become a Hollywood producer: "as a producer, I tell my writers' room not to worry if something would or would not happen in real life. We can still be authentic if what we imagine is Plausible. If you can answer credibly what realistic conditions are in place that would lead to certain decisions or actions, even if they seem out of the ordinary, the scene still works. We can defend the authenticity through plausibility." Another Agency alum counselled, "If a person in that position wouldn't normally do x in the real world, give us a reason why they would do it in your world." Don't have Agency folks save the world three times before breakfast. At least give us time to finish our coffee.

// ⊕ //

SPY-FI TRIVIA

Before you delete all of what you've learned about spying from television, novels, and the movies, here's a quick set of trivia questions about fictional spies and the actors who portrayed them:

Questions

1. Name the actor who portrayed James Bond in Woody Allen's parody of James Bond movies.

2. Name the actor who portrayed James Bond in the 1954 U.S. television show that was the first screen adaptation of an Ian Fleming-authored James Bond novel.

3. What was the title of the Woody Allen Bond film and 1954 U.S. James Bond TV show?

4. Ian Fleming named his character after the author of a book. What was the profession of the "real" James Bond?

5. Name the first six actors who played James Bond in the Broccoli series; how many Bond movies were each in?

6. Name the two actors who have portrayed Austin Powers in the *Austin Powers* movie series.

7. What four actresses have portrayed Austin Powers's sidekicks (character names and actress's names)?

8. Name the actresses who portrayed these Anne-named spy-fi icons and the TV shows in which they were depicted:

   a. Sydney Anne Bristow

   b. Annie Walker

   c. Carrie Anne Mathison

9. Name the actresses who played these spy-fi icons and the TV show or movie in which they were depicted:

   a. Nikita

   b. Evelyn Salt

   c. Lorraine Boughton

10. Name the actors/actresses who portrayed these TV spy-fi partners. Name the TV Show.

    a. Philip and Elizabeth Jennings

    b. Maxwell Smart and Agent 99 (Bonus: Who portrayed them in the movie?)

    c. Kelly Robinson and Alexander Scott (Bonus: Who portrayed them in the movie?)

    d. Napoleon Solo and Illya Kuriakin (Bonus: Who portrayed them in the movie?)

    e. John Steed and Emma Peel (Bonus: Who portrayed them in the movie?)

    f. James West and Artemus Gordon (Bonus: Who portrayed them in the movie?)

11. Name the five actors who have portrayed Jack Ryan in the movies and TV.

12. Who portrayed Matt Helm in the movie series? (Bonus: Who portrayed him in the TV series?)

13. Who portrayed Derek Flint in the movie series?

14. Who portrayed Modesty Blaise in the movie?

15. What *Star Trek* Original Series actor also appeared in the *Mission Impossible* TV series?

16. In the TV series *Archer*, what is Archer's first name?

17. Who portrays Johnny English in the movie series?

18. Who portrayed John Steed's female partners in the TV series *The Avengers*?

19. Who was John Steed's female protégé in the TV series *The New Avengers*? What actress portrayed her?

20. What were the agent numbers of:

    a. James Bond

    b. Maxwell Smart

    c. Maxwell Smart's sidekick

    d. Napoleon Solo

    e. Illya Kuriakin

    f. The Prisoner

Answers

1. David Niven

2. Barry Nelson

3. Casino Royale, which eventually was released as part of the Broccoli series

4. Ornithologist

5. Sean Connery 7; Roger Moore 7; George Lazenby 1; Timothy Dalton 2; Pierce Brosnan 4; Daniel Craig 4, as of this writing

6. Mike Myers, Tom Cruise

7. Elizabeth Hurley, Mimi Rogers: Vanessa Kensington; Heather Graham: Felicity Shagwell; Beyonce Knowles: Foxxy Cleopatra

8. a. Jennifer Garner, Alias; b. Piper Perabo, Covert Affairs; c. Claire Danes, Homeland

9. a. Maggie Q, *Nikita* 2010-2013 TV series (or Peta Wilson, who portrayed *La Femme Nikita* in the US-Canada 1997-2001 TV series; or Anne Parillaud, who portrayed Nikita/Marie Clement in the 1990 French *La Femme Nikita* movie); b. Angelina Jolie, *Salt*; c: Charlize Theron, *Atomic Blonde*

10. a. Matthew Rhys, Keri Russell, *The Americans*

    b. Don Adams and Barbara Feldon, *Get Smart* (Bonus: Steve Carell, Anne Hathaway)

    c. Robert Culp and Bill Cosby, *I Spy* (Bonus: Eddie Murphy, Owen Wilson)

    d. Robert Vaughn and David McCallum, *The Man From U.N.C.L.E.* (Bonus: Henry Cavill, Armie Hammer)

    e. Patrick McNee and Diana Rigg, *The Avengers* (Bonus: Ralph Fiennes, Uma Thurman, featuring Sean Connery)

    f. Robert Conrad, Ross Martin, *The Wild Wild West* (Bonus: Will Smith, Kevin Kline)

11. Alec Baldwin; Harrison Ford; Chris Pine; Ben Affleck; John Krasinski

12. Dean Martin (Bonus: Tony Franciosa)

13. James Coburn

14. Monica Vitti

15. Leonard Nimoy

16. Sterling

17. Rowan Atkinson

18. Honor Blackman (Cathy Gale); Diana Rigg (Emma Peel); Linda Thorson (Tara King)

19. Purdey (Joanna Lumley)

20. 20. a. 007; b. 86; c. 99; d. 1 or 11; e. 2; f. 6

FURTHER READING

There is an extensive literature on intelligence, of varying degrees of competence, authoritativeness and usefulness. Here are some that I find particularly helpful in understanding intelligence issues. You do not have to read all of these before you can comfortably write spi-fy, but this will give you a running start on developing credibility.

By all means, start with the official websites of the Intelligence Community organizations. CIA.gov is an excellent starting point for the basics, along with useful photos to orient you. Similar material is available on the rest of the IC members' sites. To keep up with current developments, I often consult TheCipherBrief.com.

Memoirs by CIA Directors

George H.W. Bush *Looking Forward: An Autobiography* New York: Bantam, 1987, 268 pp.

William Colby and Peter Forbath *Honorable Men: My Life in the CIA* New York: Simon and Schuster, 1978, 493 pp.

Allen Dulles *The Craft of Intelligence* New York: Harper and Row, 1963, 277 pp.

Robert Gates *From the Shadows: The Ultimate Insider's Story of Five Presidents and How They Won the Cold War* New York: Simon and Schuster, 1996, 604 pp.

Michael Vincent Hayden *Playing to the Edge: American Intelligence in the Age of Terror* New York: Penguin, 2016, 448 pp.

Richard Helms with William Hood *A Look Over My Shoulder: A Life in the Central Intelligence Agency* New York: Random House, 2003, 478 pp.

Michael Morell with Bill Harlow *The Great War of Our Time: The CIA's Fight from Al Qa'ida to ISIS* NY: Twelve, 2015, 395 pp.

Leon Panetta and Jim Newton *Worthy Fights: A Memoir of Leadership in War and Peace* New York: Penguin, 2014, 512 pp.

George J. Tenet with William Harlow *At the Center of the Storm: My Years at the CIA* New York: HarperCollins, 2007, 549 pp.

Stansfield Turner *Secrecy and Democracy—The CIA in Transition* Boston: Houghton Mifflin, 1985.

CIA Officers' Memoirs

Robert Baer *See No Evil: The True Story of a Ground Soldier in the CIA's War on Terrorism* New York: Crown, 2002, 284 pp., and

Robert Baer and Dayna Baer *The Company We Keep: A Husband-and-Wife True-Life Spy Story* New York: Crown, 2011, 320 pp.

Nada Bakos with Davin Coburn *The Targeter: My Life in the CIA, on the Hunt for the Godfather of ISIS* New York: Little, Brown, 2019, 368 pp.

Milt Bearden and James Risen *The Main Enemy: The Inside Story of the CIA's Final Showdown with the KGB* New York: Random House, 2003, 506 pp.

Glenn Carle *The Interrogator: An Education* New York: Nation Books, 2012, 336 pp.

Duane R. Clarridge *A Spy for All Seasons: My Life in the CIA* New York: Scribner, 1996, 430 pp.

Miles Copeland *The Game Player: Confessions of the CIA's Original Political Operative* London: Aurum Press, 1989.

Henry Crumpton *The Art of Intelligence: Lessons From a Life in the CIA's Clandestine Service* New York: Penguin, 2013, 352 pp.

William J. Daugherty *In the Shadow of the Ayatollah: A CIA Hostage in Iran* Annapolis, Maryland: Naval Institute Press, 2001, 280 pp.

Jack Devine with Vernon Loeb *Good Hunting: An American Spymaster's Story* New York: Farrar, Straus and Giroux, 2014, 333 pp.

Lawrence Devlin *Chief of Station/Congo: Fighting the Cold War in a Hot Zone* New York: Public Affairs, 2008, 312 pp.

Tom Gilligan *CIA Life: 10,000 Days with the Agency* Guilford, Connecticut: Foreign Intelligence Press, 1991, 285 pp.

Austin Goodrich *Born to Spy: Recollections of a CIA Case Officer* New York: iUniverse, 2004, 157 pp.

Donald Gregg *Pot Shards: Fragments of a Life Lived in CIA, the White House, and the Two Koreas* Washington, D.C.: New Academia Publishing/Vellum Books, 2014, 346 pp.

Robert L. Grenier *88 Days to Kandahar: A CIA Diary* New York: Simon and Schuster, 2015, 465 pp.

Howard Philips Hart *A Life for a Life: A Memoir: My Career in Espionage Working for the Central Intelligence Agency* Lulu Press, 2015, 148 pp.

Richard Holm *The American Agent: My Life in the CIA* London: St. Ermin's Press, 2003, 462 pp.

Richard Holm and Timothy Miller *The Craft We Chose: My Life in the CIA* Mountain Lake Park, Maryland: Mountain Lake Press, 2011, 584 pp.

Jack Kassinger *Holding Hands with Heroes* Dorrance Publishing, 2010, 256 pp.

Bina C. Kiyonaga *My Spy: Memoir of a CIA Wife* New York: Harper Perennial, 2001, 336 pp.

Chris Lynch *The CI Desk: FBI and CIA Counterintelligence As Seen From My Cubicle* Dog Ear Publishing, 2010.

Melissa Boyle Mahle *Denial and Deception: An Insider's View of the CIA* New York: Nation Books, 2005, 418 pp.

Edward Mickolus, ed. *Stories from Langley: A Glimpse Inside the CIA* Washington, D.C., and Lincoln, Nebraska: Potomac Books/University of Nebraska Press, 2014, 387 pp.

Edward Mickolus, ed. *More Stories from Langley: Another Glimpse Inside the CIA* Washington, D.C., and Lincoln, Nebraska: Potomac Books/University of Nebraska Press, 2020.

Floyd L. Paseman *A Spy's Journey: A CIA Memoir* St. Paul: Zenith Press, 2004, 287 pp.

Shirley H. Perry *After Many Days* Hellgate Press, 2010, 197 pp.

Martha Peterson *The Widow Spy* Red Canary Press, 2012, 262 pp.

David Atlee Phillips *The Night Watch: 25 Years of Peculiar Service* New York: Atheneum, 1977.

David Atlee Phillips *Secret Wars Diary: My Adventures in Combat, Espionage Operations and Covert Action* Bethesda, Maryland: Stone Trail Press, 1989, 343 pp.

John Rizzo *Company Man: 30 Years of Controversy and Crisis in the CIA* NY: Scribner 2014, 338 pp.

Jose A. Rodriguez, Jr. with Bill Harlow *Hard Measures: How Aggressive CIA Actions After 9/11 Saved American Lives* New York: Threshold Editions, 2013, 304 pp.

Ted Shackley with Richard A. Finney *Spymaster: My Life in the CIA* Dulles, Virginia: Potomac Books, 2005, 309 pp.

J. Perry Smith *The Unlikely Priest* Jacksonville, Florida: Padre Nuestro, 2011, 280 pp.

TJ Waters *Class 11: Inside the CIA's First Post-9/11 Spy Class* New York: Dutton, 2006, 320 pp.

Valerie Plame Wilson *Fair Game: My Life as a Spy, My Betrayal by the White House* New York: Simon and Schuster, 2007.

Analysis

John Helgerson *Getting to Know the President: CIA Briefings of Presidential Candidates, 1952-1992* Washington, D.C.: Center for Study of Intelligence, CIA, 1995.

Richards J. Heuer *Psychology of Intelligence Analysis* Pherson Associates, 2007.

Richards J. Heuer, Jr., ed. *Quantitative Approaches to Political Intelligence: The CIA Experience* Boulder, Colorado: Westview Press, 1978.

Richards J. Heuer and Randolph Pherson *Structured Analytical Techniques for Intelligence Analysis* CQ Press, 2014, 384 pp.

Edward Mickolus *Briefing for the Boardroom and the Situation Room* Washington, D.C.: Daniel Morgan Academy, 2015, 70 pp.

David Priess *The President's Book of Secrets: The Untold Story of Intelligence Briefings to America's Presidents* Public Affairs, 2017, 400 pp.

Science and Technology

Dino Brugioni *Eyeball to Eyeball: The Inside Story of the Cuban Missile Crisis* New York: Random House, 1990.

Antonio J. Mendez with Malcolm McConnell *The Master of Disguise: My Secret Life in the CIA* New York: Perennial, 1999, 351 pp.

Antonio and Jonna Mendez with Bruce Henderson *Spy Dust: Two Masters of Disguise Reveal the Tools and Operations That Helped Win the Cold War* New York: Atria Books, 2002, 306 pp.

David Robarge *Archangel* Washington, D.C.: Center for the Study of Intelligence, 2007.

Kevin Ruffner, ed. *CORONA: America's First Satellite Program* Washington, D.C.: CIA History Staff, 1995.

Robert Wallace and H. Keith Melton with Henry R. Schlesinger *Spycraft: The Secret History of the CIA's Spytechs, from Communism to Al-Qaeda* New York: Plume, 2009, 576 pp.

Counterintelligence

Sandra Grimes and Jeanne Vertefeuille *Circle of Treason: A CIA Account of Traitor Aldrich Ames and the Men He Betrayed* Annapolis, Maryland: Naval Institute Press, 2012.

Edward Mickolus *The Counterintelligence Chronology: Spying by and Against the United States from the 1700s through 2014* Jefferson, North Carolina: McFarland, 2015, 233 pp.

James Olson *To Catch a Spy: The Art of Counterintelligence* Washington, D.C.: Georgetown University Press, 2019

Michael J. Sulick *American Spies: Espionage Against the United States from the Cold War to the Present* Washington, D.C.: Georgetown University Press, 2013, 370 pp.

Michael J. Sulick *Spying in America: Espionage from the Revolutionary War to the Dawn of the Cold War* Washington, D.C.: Georgetown University Press, 2012, 320 pp.

Robert Wallace, H. Keith Melton and Henry R. Schlesinger *Spy Sites of New York City* The Foreign Excellent Trenchcoat Society, 2012, 160 pp.

Supporting Operations and Analysis

Philip Houston, Michael Floyd and Susan Carnicero, with Don Tennant *Get the Truth: Former CIA Officers Teach You How to Persuade Anyone to Tell All* NY: St. Martin's, 2015, 272 pp.

Richard G. Irwin *KH601: And Ye Shall Know the Truth and the Truth Shall Make You Free: My Life in the Central Intelligence Agency* Virginia: Fortis, 2010, 372 pp.

John F. Sullivan *Gatekeeper: Memoirs of a CIA Polygraph Examiner* Washington, D.C.: Potomac, 2007, 273 pp.

John F. Sullivan *Of Spies and Lies: A CIA Lie Detector Remembers Vietnam* Lawrence: University Press of Kansas, 2002, 250 pp.

Overviews of Intelligence Culture and Humor

Roger Hall *You're Stepping on My Cloak and Dagger* New York: W. W. Norton, 1957, 219 pp.

Charles E. Lathrop *The Literary Spy: The Ultimate Source for Quotations on Espionage and Intelligence* New Haven: Yale University Press, 2004, 496 pp.

Edward Mickolus *The Secret Book of CIA Humor* Gretna, Louisiana, Pelican, 2011, 240 pp.

Edward Mickolus *The Secret Book of Intelligence Community Humor* Ponte Vedra, Florida: Wandering Woods, 2018, 190 pp.

Edward Mickolus *Two Spies Walk Into a Bar* Ponte Vedra, Florida: Wandering Woods, 2018, 188 pp.

Tom Sileo *CIA Humor: A Few True Stories from a 31-Year Career* Alexandria, Virginia: Washington House, 2004, 101 pp.

James Olson *Fair Play: The Moral Dilemmas of Spying* Washington, D.C.: Potomac, 2006, 291 pp.

Intelligence Community

Douglas F. Garthoff *Directors of Central Intelligence as Leaders of the U.S. Intelligence Community — 1946-2005* Washington, D.C.: Center for the Study of Intelligence, 2005.

Mark Lowenthal *Intelligence: From Secrets to Policy*, 7th edition CQ Press, 2016, 624 pp.

Hollywood Portrayals

Nicholas Dujmovic "Getting CIA History Right: The Informal Partnership Between Agency Historians and Outside Scholars" 26, 2-3 *Intelligence and National Security* April-June 2011, pp 228-245.

Nicholas Dujmovic "Hollywood, Don't You Go Disrespectin' My Culture: The Good Shepherd Versus Real CIA History" 23, 1 *Intelligence and National Security* February 2008, pp. 25-41.

Fiction

Susan Hasler *Intelligence: A Novel of the CIA* Thomas Dunne Books, 2010, 320 pp.

Jason Matthews *The Kremlin's Candidate* NY: Scribner, 2018, 448 pp.

Jason Matthews *Palace of Treason* NY: Scribner, 2015, 496 pp.

Jason Matthews *Red Sparrow* NY: Scribner, 2014, 576 pp. Read the book; the movie did not do it justice.

T.L. Williams *Cooper's Revenge* Ponte Vedra: First Coast Publishers, 2013, 251 pp.

T.L. Williams *Unit 400: The Assassins* Ponte Vedra: First Coast Publishers, 2014, 288 pp.

T.L. Williams *Zero Day: China's Cyber Wars* Ponte Vedra: First Coast Publishers, 2015, 346 pp.

T.L. Williams *The Last Caliph* Ponte Vedra: First Coast Publishers, 2019, 370 pp.

ABOUT THE AUTHOR

D r. Edward Mickolus, after graduating from Georgetown University, wrote the first doctoral dissertation on international terrorism while earning an M.A., M.Phil, and Ph.D. from Yale University.

He then served in analytical, operational, management, and staff positions in the Central Intelligence Agency for 33 years, where he was CIA's first full-time analyst on international terrorism; analyzed African political, economic, social, military, and leadership issues; wrote political-psychological assessments of world leaders; and managed collection, counterintelligence, and covert action programs against terrorists, drug traffickers, weapons proliferators, and hostile espionage services.

He founded Vinyard Software, Inc., whose products include IT-ERATE (International Terrorism: Attributes of Terrorist Events) text and numeric datasets and DOTS (Data on Terrorist Suspects). Clients include 200 universities in two dozen countries.

His 40 books include a series of multi-volume chronologies and biographies on international terrorism; more than two dozen book chapters; 100 articles and reviews in refereed scholarly journals and newspapers and presentations to professional societies; and 14 humorous publications.

For the following ten years, he was a senior instructor for SAIC and its spinoff, Leidos, Inc. He served as the Deborah M. Hixon Professor of Intelligence Tradecraft and Board of Advisors member at the Daniel Morgan Graduate School in Washington, D.C. and teaches at the University of North Florida and Jacksonville University.

Books by Ed Mickolus

America's Funniest Memes: Coronavirus Edition

More Stories From Langley: Another Glimpse Inside the CIA

Terrorism Worldwide, 2018

His Words

The Secret Book of Intelligence Community Humor

Two Spies Walk Into a Bar

Terrorism Worldwide, 2017

Terrorism Worldwide, 2016

Terrorism 2013-2015: A Worldwide Chronology

Briefing for the Boardroom and the Situation Room

The Counterintelligence Chronology: Spying by and Against the United States from the 1700s through 2014

Food with Thought: The Wit and Wisdom of Chinese Fortune Cookies

Stories from Langley: A Glimpse Inside the CIA

with Susan L. Simmons *The 50 Worst Terrorist Attacks*

Terrorism 2008-2012: A Worldwide Chronology

with Joseph T. Brannan *Coaching Winning Model United Nations Teams*

The Secret Book of CIA Humor

with Susan L. Simmons *The Terrorist List: North America*

with Susan L. Simmons *The Terrorist List: South America*

with Susan L. Simmons *The Terrorist List: Eastern Europe*

with Susan L. Simmons *The Terrorist List: Western Europe*

with Susan L. Simmons *The Terrorist List: Asia, Pacific, and Sub-Saharan Africa*

The Terrorist List: The Middle East, 2 volumes

Terrorism, 2005-2007

with Susan L. Simmons *Terrorism, 2002-2004: A Chronology*, 3 volumes

with Susan L. Simmons *Terrorism, 1996-2001: A Chronology of Events and a Selectively Annotated Bibliography*, 2 volumes

with Susan L. Simmons *Terrorism, 1992-1995: A Chronology of Events and a Selectively Annotated Bibliography*

Terrorism, 1988-1991: A Chronology of Events and a Selectively Annotated Bibliography

with Todd Sandler and Jean Murdock *International Terrorism in the 1980s: A Chronology, Volume 2: 1984-1987*

with Todd Sandler and Jean Murdock *International Terrorism in the 1980s: A Chronology, Volume 1: 1980-1983*

with Peter Flemming *Terrorism, 1980-1987: A Selectively Annotated Bibliography*

International Terrorism: Attributes of Terrorist Events, 1968-1977, ITER-ATE 2 Data Codebook

The Literature of Terrorism: A Selectively Annotated Bibliography

Transnational Terrorism: A Chronology of Events, 19681979

ITERATE: International Terrorism: Attributes of Terrorist Events, Data Codebook

Combatting International Terrorism: A Quantitative Analysis

with Joseph Rendon *Take My Weight… Please!*

with Harlan Rector *I Matter: Finding Meaning in Your Life at Any Age, volume 1*

with Harlan Rector *I Matter Too: Finding Meaning in Your Life at Any Age, volume 2 (forthcoming)*

Terrorism Worldwide 2019-2020 (forthcoming)

More Funny 2020 Covid Memes (forthcoming)

with Tracy Tripp *White Noise Whispers*

www.ingramcontent.com/pod-product-compliance
Lightning Source LLC
Chambersburg PA
CBHW060244030426
42335CB00014B/1597